WALTER GRAEBNER

*My dear*
MISTER
CHURCHILL

LONDON
MICHAEL JOSEPH

*First published by*
MICHAEL JOSEPH LTD
*26 Bloomsbury Street*
*London, W.C.1*
1965

To C.L.G.

*Set and printed in Great Britain by Tonbridge Printers Ltd,*
*Peach Hall Works, Tonbridge, Kent, in Baskerville eleven on*
*thirteen point, on paper made by Henry Bruce at Currie,*
*Midlothian, and bound by James Burn at Esher, Surrey*

# CONTENTS

# ILLUSTRATIONS

The author thanks *Life* magazine for
permission to reproduce a number of photographs.
The frontispiece is by William Sumits—*Life*

# INTRODUCTION

I T was some time in 1948 that I got the idea of writing
a short book about Mr Churchill. In the previous few
years I had come to know him fairly well, and from
time to time, after a visit to Chartwell, his country home
in Kent, or to his town house in London, I would describe
an incident or relate an anecdote to some of my friends.
One day someone said: 'I hope you are keeping notes,
because hardly anyone has had the good luck to spend so
much time in the presence of the great man. You are
assembling a footnote to history, and you must see that it
gets into print.' Although I had not kept notes, I began
thinking about the suggestion, and in 1950 I spent the
whole of my summer holiday in the Italian Alps writing
down almost everything that I could remember. I showed
the notes to a number of people, including several publishers, and the interest they showed encouraged me to go
forward with the project.

In the years that followed I often felt that I could never
bring myself to publish anything about a man of such
incomparable stature. 'Who am I,' I said to myself, 'to try
to tell what he was like? Only an eminent historian could
do justice to the subject.' Nevertheless, I continued, putting
off the final decision about publication until later. The
only definite decision I took was that, if I published anything at all, I would not have it appear while Mr Churchill
was alive.

One morning at 10 Downing Street, during a bedside conversation about books, I managed to pluck up enough courage to tell the Prime Minister that I was working on a book about him, which would be a record of impressions that I had formed over the years. His reaction, though it left me in no doubt as to his approval of what I was doing, did not exactly inflate my ego as an author. 'Very good,' he said, with a gleam in his eyes, 'You should get Rufie to help you.' Rufie was a little brown poodle I had given to Mr Churchill some years earlier, and was lying on the bed at the time we were talking.

A few days before Christmas in 1953 I had a conversation with an Englishwoman in London which, more than anything else, helped me to make up my mind about publication. 'Of course, publish it,' she said, 'and have it ready to appear as soon after his death as possible. The only thing that matters is *what* you write, and since you admire him so much, surely you must go ahead with it.'

The story that follows is about a man so great that I suppose another like him will not live in the next century, a man that no one could know without loving. I shall always be aware of my good fortune, especially since I am a citizen of another country, in having had the opportunity of getting to know him.

As I believe he will be remembered best as Mr Churchill, and since that was his name during most of the time I knew him, I am not using the title Sir Winston. Likewise I am calling Lady Churchill Mrs Churchill for the same reason.

*My dear*
MISTER
CHURCHILL

# CHAPTER ONE

# CHURCHILL

## AND I

ABOUT a month after the British General Election of 1945 I had my first appointment with Mr Churchill, and there was no particular reason why it should not have been my last. As things turned out the meeting marked the beginning of an association which for a number of years brought me into his company as often probably as anyone outside his family, his closest circle of friends, immediate staff and governmental colleagues.

Some weeks earlier I had been asked by the editors of *Life* Magazine to approach Churchill about writing a series of three articles, for which they were prepared to pay $75,000. I wrote him a short letter, received a courteous but negative reply from his secretary, and forgot about the whole business.

Then one day Randolph Churchill, whom I knew slightly, invited me to meet him at the Ritz Bar. 'Father would like to see you,' he said at once. 'I think he's got something to show you that will interest you. Do you remember the letter you wrote to him a short while back? It's about that that he wants to see you. He's at Claridges. Ring Miss Hill to fix a time.'

I went to Churchill's apartment on the top floor of

Claridges the next day at twelve. Miss Hill opened the
door and asked me to take a seat in the drawing-room to
the left, adding, 'Mr Churchill will be here in a moment.'
I looked for a chair, but none was empty. Every chair and
sofa in the room had a painting on it, so there was nothing
for me to do but wander around and examine the collection.

Here was showmanship at its best. Churchill had carefully set up a private exhibition, and I was his audience.
Just as I had finished inspecting the last of about a dozen
pictures, Churchill walked in wearing his blue zip suit, his
face pink and powdery after a shave, his pale blue eyes
smiling.

'I've been on holiday in Italy and the South of France
as you may know,' he began, 'and while there I made
these paintings which you see—er—in this gallery—on
private view. You wrote to me a short time ago about
writing some articles——'

Marching up and down the room he continued: 'That
was a very good offer you made me—very flattering—I
wish I could have accepted it. It's the best offer I've ever
had. Five dollars a word I think it works out at. That's
very good. But I am not in a position to write anything
now—perhaps later—but not now. I have gone into the
whole thing very carefully with my advisors and they tell
me that if I come out of retirement—you see I've been
in retirement ever since the election when the people
turned me out—and write anything now I would have to
pay taxes of nineteen and six in the pound, so what's the
use?'

Then, gesturing towards the paintings, he concluded:
'But these are something else again. Do you think your
people might like to publish *them*—that is, to take them in

place of one of the articles. I would like such an arrangement better for the time being, as the income, I am
advised, would be considered as a capital gain and therefore non-taxable.'

The point was clear. Churchill was offering for $25,000
the reproduction rights to the paintings he had made on
holiday. It was agreed that I would communicate with my
editors. Before leaving I congratulated him on the excel-
lence of his pictures, expressing surprise that he could find
the time to take up painting on top of all his other work.
Behind an enormous grin he murmured: 'Genius has many
outlets.'

Some weeks later arrangements were made to publish
the pictures, and their appearance helped to intensify the
interest in amateur painting which was then beginning to
capture the U.S.

A month or so afterwards, I was asked to go one morning
to 28 Hyde Park Gate, Kensington, the town house of the
Churchills. Sawyers, who was valet at that time, showed
me upstairs, opened a door to a large bedroom, and
intoned: 'Mr Graebner, Sir.' I walked through the door
that Sawyers held open for me, and saw propped up in a
huge bed the figure of Mr Churchill, wrapped in a colour-
ful Chinese dressing gown. 'Good morning,' he said. 'It's
so good of you to come. Please have a seat. Would you like
a whisky and soda?' So began the first of many conferences
in this bedroom-office at No. 28.

Stacked in front of Mr Churchill on a small tray-like
table was a thick manuscript on which his fingers rested
lightly. 'I have here some very secret documents,' he said,
peering at me over his heavy black-rimmed spectacles. 'I
am going to read to you from them, but all that you hear

must be kept in the strictest confidence.' He then added with a light chuckle: 'We might be liable to prosecution under the Official Secrets Act if we're not careful.'

The demonstration, complete with tears and gestures, was magnificent, and lasted for about an hour. When it was over Churchill explained that he had been reading from speeches he had delivered in the wartime Secret Sessions of Parliament. Then he offered the publication rights to the organization that I was representing.

Churchill was highly pleased with the results, and a year later, when the speeches came out in book form, he found an opportunity of recognizing the small role I had played. I was spending a wintry afternoon with him in his study at Chartwell while he was autographing copies of the book for various friends and dignitaries. 'And here's one to sign for the King of ——,' said the secretary on duty. It was a beautiful gilt-edged edition bound in rich red leather. Churchill puffed at his cigar, looked around at his secretary, and said: 'I think we'll give this copy to Mr Graebner.'

His next overture came in the spring of 1947. I had just left the night train from Paris at Geneva and was registering at a hotel when a bellboy said to me, 'London is calling you.' Churchill was on the line. He began talking in the same easy, matter-of-fact way in which he addressed his secretaries on the house telephones. 'That was a momentous speech Truman made yesterday,' he said. 'By this action America may save the world. It may mean peace.'

I did not know what on earth he was talking about as I hadn't seen the morning papers as yet. My reply, whatever it was, made no sense, but that was unimportant because Churchill often did not listen to what others said over the

telephone, and this fortunately was such a time. He went on: 'A very bold and courageous idea. I think I would like to write an article about it. Would your people be interested? I cannot promise that I *will* write an article, as I may find after starting it that I can't finish it, but I'll try, and if I can do it at all it will be finished by Saturday.'

When the call ended I sent for a newspaper, and there, of course, was the story on the front page: THE TRUMAN DOCTRINE. The United States had in effect served notice on Russia that it would resist aggression in Greece, Turkey and elsewhere in the Eastern Mediterranean.

The following Saturday afternoon I went to Chartwell, and found Churchill putting the final touches to the article. A few days later it was being read around the world.

Churchill's main literary activity after the war was, of course, his *Memoirs*, and while one volume after another was being produced—until there were six in all—I saw him constantly.

There seemed always something to be discussed or something that Churchill wanted, and like everyone else closely connected with him—whether horse-trainer, bookie, doctor, fellow cabinet minister or valet—I soon got used to frequent telephone calls from 'Westerham 81.' They came at almost any hour of the day or night and usually were a summons for me to appear at Chartwell for a meal or a drink within a few hours' time.

At these sessions Churchill usually had some questions relating directly or indirectly to the *Memoirs* to discuss, but sometimes the point was so unimportant that he had difficulty in remembering it when I arrived. Once the only thing that he seemed to want of me was a refill for his gold ball-point pen which he liked for correcting

galleys. He thought I might be able to get him one in New York.

Most of the time, however, there was something on his mind about the book. About once a month he asked me to Chartwell or Hyde Park Gate simply to tell me how the current work was progressing. Sometimes he would read extracts to me and then enlarge at great length on what he had written; at other times, while he dressed, bathed, or talked to almost anyone from Anthony Eden to his horse-trainer on the telephone, I would read a chapter or two that he had just finished. He always watched for my reaction, and if I finished a chapter too quickly he was a little annoyed, probably because he thought that I was bored and was not reading carefully.

He soon came to treat me almost as one of his own staff, with the functions of sounding-board and test-tube of reader reaction. I was often put hard to work. Once I was handed a massive pile of galleys, totalling some 400,000 words, and told: 'I would be very glad if you'd read these and let me have your comments in writing. Don't try to read both books at one sitting. You'd get too tired. Read four or five hours at a time. That's the only way to read.'

Again, while I was on holiday with him in Marrakech, he would give me a set of proofs late in the evening, asking for my reaction. By nine o'clock next morning his secretary would be on the phone to inquire if I had finished. 'Mr Churchill is ready now for your comments,' she would say, 'and would like the proofs back.'

Of course, though he wanted to know what I thought of his writings, he did not necessarily pay much attention to my views, or, indeed, to those of anyone ese. But he liked to feel that everyone round him was working as hard on

the *Memoirs*, and was as interested in them as he was himself.

During these years I saw him at least once every two weeks, and spent many days with him on his holidays. I was with him twice at Marrakech in French Morocco, once at Aix-en-Provence in Southern France, and once at Monte Carlo.

During his second Prime Ministership, from 1951 to 1955, I continued to see him from time to time at Chequers, the official country residence of British Prime Ministers, at 10 Downing Street and at Chartwell. Since his *Memoirs* were almost finished, there was very little business for us to conduct during this period, and in consequence I was always especially flattered to receive an invitation from him.

One day he asked me to come to Chartwell while he was convalescing from the stroke in June, 1953. Rumours of all kinds had been flying around London about his health, so I did not know quite what to expect as I waited with two other luncheon guests for him to enter the drawing-room to greet us. At 1.30 he shuffled in, perhaps a little less sure-footed than usual, but otherwise gay and smiling happily. He was wearing one of his zip or siren suits, a greyish-blue flannel with a pin stripe. A minute or two later we went into lunch.

As he poured champagne into my glass he said: 'My illness, though it should have been mortal, never prevented me from having a square meal and a pint of champagne to go with it.' Later he said that for a time he had lost the use of both legs, and that one arm was partially paralysed.

He was anxious to know how I thought he appeared, and when I told him that I couldn't detect any big change he seemed pleased, and boasted proudly, 'This decaying

B

carcass can still bring fame to anything, so long as it's not overworked.' He was particularly worried about his speech which had developed a slight huskiness. 'I will decide in the next few weeks whether to stay on the job or not,' he announced, then, with eyes twinkling, added: 'It's easy enough to get out, but it's a devil of a lot harder to come back in once you're out.'

In the late afternoon he asked me to go with him for a walk in the gardens. Though it was then five o'clock and the afternoon was getting cold and damp, there were forty or fifty people standing on a little hillock outside the gates waiting to catch a glimpse of the great man as he emerged. They cheered loudly, and Churchill responded with the familiar broad smile and 'V' sign. We fed the goldfish, and then we sat down on a bench from which we could see the whole weald of Kent unfold towards the sea. From time to time Rufie brought a ball which he asked his master to throw for him, and in between throws Churchill thought aloud about the future. 'I must be sure that I can master the House of Commons. I'm not worried about anything else, but if I can't master the House I must not go on.'

The next year was one of the busiest in his life, and many of his friends thought that the stimulation he derived from all the political activity helped greatly to keep him alive. He flew the Atlantic twice to see President Eisenhower, guided Anthony Eden through some very stormy waters at the Geneva Conference on Indo-China, and got the House of Commons to do just what he wanted, though many of the debates lasted all night. When I saw him at Chartwell just after the House had risen for the 1954 summer recess, he talked a little of his exhausting life as a peacetime Prime Minister. 'In many ways I had an easier time of it during

the war,' he said. 'Then, if we won a battle, we simply began preparing for the next. If we lost one, it was the same. We always knew exactly where we stood, and we had the power to act as we thought best. Now everything is different. There is so much patter, patter, patter, chatter, chatter, chatter, it's a wonder anything ever gets done.'

That same afternoon Churchill indicated to me for the first time that he was seriously thinking of retiring. Somehow he led the conversation round to holidays, saying: 'I've been thinking a lot about Marrakech lately. I don't believe there's a better place to go to.' When I agreed, and said that in my opinion February was the best month there, he looked at me in the teasing way that was characteristic of him and said: 'Do you mean the best month for me to retire?'

After his final departure from No. 10 in April, 1955, Churchill withdrew almost completely from active, on-stage politics, and quietly slid back into the kind of life he had led between 1945 and 1950. He plunged into last-minute revisions and additional chapters to his *History of the English Speaking Peoples*, collected various awards, and again took out his paint brushes and easels. But before he organized himself and his staff of secretaries and assistants for the last retirement, he worked day and night for weeks to help Anthony Eden and the Conservatives win the Election.

It was right in the middle of the campaign that I took some American friends of mine out to Chartwell one Sunday for tea. Since Mr Churchill was so pressed we had arranged to walk around the estate by ourselves, and then meet one of the secretaries in the drawing-room. After we had settled down to our second cup, third sand-

wich and second bun, and had long since given up any
hope of catching even a glimpse of the famous man, the
door suddenly opened and in he shuffled, with hand outstretched, cheeks pink and eyes bright, if a little red. After
greeting everyone and welcoming my friends with a warmth
that might well have been reserved for important dignitaries, he apologized for not having been with us earlier,
then said: 'I've got to make five speeches in the next week.
That's a big job. But just this minute I finished all the
uphill work. Now I can coast. Won't you have something
to drink? And a cigar?' There followed half an hour of talk
during which Churchill was at the peak of his form as he
flitted from a barb at the Russians one moment to a serious
inquiry as to the state of American business the next.

Before very long the London newspapers were full of
criticisms of the Government and were forecasting the
early resignation of Prime Minister Eden. So I made up
my mind that I would sound out Mr Churchill on the
subject. Over the years I had learned that a general
reference was sometimes enough to get him started. On
this occasion he appeared at first not to understand what
I was talking about. When I tried again he merely stared
at me and made a few noises which I could not follow. My
third effort was a direct question: 'What's going to happen
to Sir Anthony?' Mr Churchill thought for a moment,
looked at me, and said: 'Well, they're having a good
gallop.' Clearly he did not wish to continue the discussion,
and took the first opportunity to ask about the health of
Mr Eisenhower. 'I was terribly shocked when he became
ill,' he said. 'He's been a fine President at a most difficult
and important period in history. I do hope he will make a
complete recovery.'

During the last years of his life I hardly saw Mr Churchill at all. My last conversation with him took place at Claridges where we first met, and where Lord Beaverbrook was giving a dinner party for the Prime Ministers of the Atlantic Provinces of Canada. At that time he was already very frail, and his hearing had become extremely difficult. I sat quietly next to him for a few minutes before the dinner began, and managed after a while to interest him a little in the subject of Rufie. Having learned no more than that Rufie still liked to chase balls I decided that Mr Churchill was in no mood to talk and probably wanted to be left alone with his own thoughts.

# CHAPTER TWO

## CHURCHILL

## THE HOST

NEARLY everyone imagines that Winston Churchill, the leading citizen of the western world in his time, would have been a slightly terrifying person to meet. What could one talk about to interest such a great man? And when he spoke how on earth could one respond? Obviously one could not engage in small talk about the weather, or the social season in London, with such a personage; and it might seem almost impertinence to bandy views on the great questions of the day. I have known many distinguished people who, when they went to meet him for the first time, were in an ecstasy of excitement and terror, and who in his presence became more like bashful schoolboys taking tea with the headmaster than self-assured men of the world paying their respects to a famous person.

Yet, though his fame could not help but raise a certain barrier between himself and his guests, no man tried harder than Churchill to put even his least important visitors at their ease. He greeted them invariably with a broad, kindly smile and a hand outstretched for several seconds as he walked up to them. His clasp was firm and hearty, his words of welcome unfailingly warm. And the famous

zip suit he customarily wore (striped worsted for lunch, black velvet for dinner) struck from the beginning that note of informality which would continue throughout the visit.

So a guest of Winston Churchill could relax, that is, if he were wise enough to let Churchill dominate the proceedings completely, and clever enough to toss back the few stray conversational balls that came his way. For no matter who was there, it was always Churchill's show. And a good show too.

He it was who decided every topic of conversation and changed it whenever it suited him, skipping from subject to subject and back again with a dexterity which would sometimes leave his audience breathless, but always spellbound. Anything that came to him on the spur of the moment was grist for him, whether serious or gay, whether anecdote or song or poem.

Sometimes at dinner he would start off the talk with his views on Communism. There always followed a bitter denunciation. 'The blood of the Communists flows green,' he would hiss. Or he might hold forth for half an hour on a point of history. Shortly after he began his *Memoirs*, I remember, he somehow got interested in a book describing past invasions of China. He had evidently spent most of the preceding night with the volume and next day at luncheon recounted with delight innumerable facts and figures on the number of ships taking part, the length of the crossings, the casualty figures, etc.—all, apparently, with the most amazing accuracy.

As Prime Minister, his conversation would often take a functional turn: he would seek information or reactions on matters that might influence Government policy. At a

lunch at Chequers one day, he suddenly stopped all conversation by calling to me across the table: 'How many college graduates are there in the United States?' I hazarded a guess—between five and six million. 'I would have thought there were about fifteen,' said Churchill, 'but anyway there are a great many, and yet the country produces 103 million tons of steel.' He was obviously preparing to answer the old fallacy that the more you educate people, the fewer workers you will have and the lower will be your production of raw materials.

Sometimes one would be given a glimpse of his political wisdom. 'It is not the weak country that is most likely to be attacked,' he told me once at Chequers. 'The real danger is to be strong, *but not strong enough*. If you are weak, the enemy power will probably leave you alone. It does not fear you, and it can deal with you at any time. But if you are moderately strong, and are becoming stronger every day, the enemy may well strike while he still can.'

But even as Prime Minister he always seemed, in his table conversation, to take more delight in playing with whimsical and fantastic ideas than in discussing the stern problems of the moment. I remember a lunch at Downing Street at a time when he was in the middle of a parliamentary crisis. He arrived late because of the press of business, and left early in order to defend himself and his party against a Labour vote of censure. But while at the table he was able to relax completely and soon soared off into a dissertation on God, the world and the hereafter that kept us spellbound for many minutes.

He started off by describing the early days of aviation in the First World War, telling us that no one ever dreamed of using planes for anything but reconnaissance until one

day a pilot just happened to have his rifle with him, took a pot-shot at an enemy pilot and so began aerial warfare.

'I wonder what God thinks of the things His creatures have invented,' he reflected. 'Really, it's surprising He has allowed it—but then I suppose He has so many things to think of, not only us, but all His worlds. I wouldn't have His job for anything. Mine is hard enough, but His is much more difficult. And—umph—He can't even resign.

'You know, most people are going to be very surprised when they get to Heaven. They are looking forward to meeting fascinating people like Napoleon and Julius Cæsar. But they'll probably never even be able to find them, because there will be so many millions of other people there too—Indians and Chinamen and people like that. Everyone will have equal rights in Heaven. That will be the real Welfare State.

'And then there will be the cherubs. How strange it will be to have them around. Do you know the story of the French priest who was so holy that one day in his church he saw fluttering above him a throng of cherubs. He was not only holy, but polite, and begged them to sit down. "*Mais*," replied the cherubs, "*nous n'avons pas de quoi.*" '

Any chance remark might call forth an aphorism which one could see slowly taking shape in his mind—from the sudden gleam in his eyes through the pauses and grunts and broadening grin to the triumphant end. On a point of grammar, I remember him saying, 'Splitting an infinitive isn't so bad—not nearly so bad—hmph, as splitting a Party. That is always regarded as the greatest sin.' Or at cigar time: 'Tobacco is bad for love; but old age is worse.' Or, in a more serious vein: 'I have a remedy for worries that always works. Never let one worry, no matter how

great, be in your mind all alone. It will drive you mad. Give it company, preferably something smaller, and write it down on a piece of paper. Then you will spend some time thinking about the second worry, and the first one will gradually diminish.'

Sometimes he would break out into song, usually at Mrs Churchill's prompting. Mostly it was an old army or school song that he had learned many years before, and he would sing it desperately off-key in a hoarse bass voice. Sometimes, he would suddenly start to quote the poetry he loved. He had an incredible memory—one of the reasons for his genius—and if something reminded him of Tennyson it was nothing for him to recite a hundred lines or more of *Locksley Hall*. I remember one luncheon when for a good ten minutes he repeated passages from Siegfried Sassoon's war poems. At the end his eyes were filled with tears. Poetry moved him deeply, as did any stirring or tragic tale. And it was an extraordinary and deeply impressive sight to see the old man quietly weeping into his pudding while the guests looked on, somehow not a bit abashed, and Mrs Churchill, at her end of the table, quietly took up a new line of conversation.

Occasionally he would amuse himself by making up a few lines of doggerel verse on the spur of the moment. Once when we were discussing the sleeping pills, which both he and I had to take occasionally, he turned with an impish grin to my wife and intoned:

'Your husband is a very temperate man—hmph
He needs—er—a little sedative to sleep.'

Then, quickly and victoriously:

'He should drink all the brandy that he can—hmph
You've really very little cause to weep.'

At another time, in Morocco, he burst forth with a
fractured-French critique of painting:

> *'La peinture á l'huile*
> *Est bien difficile.*
> *Mais c'est aussi plus beau*
> *Que la peinture á l'eau.'*

Then at other times many minutes would pass without
his saying a word. He would become completely oblivious
to everyone else in the room, close his eyes, hold his head
in his hands and screw up his face as if in pain or in deep,
agonizing thought. At such times he would often talk to
himself, in a half whisper.

These moods never lasted long. After a minute or two
he would snap out of them and again take over the conversation. But a few minutes later he might again be silent.
There were times, too, when he would simply close his
eyes in front of his guests and go to sleep, not because he
was bored, but only because he was very tired. When he
awoke he always felt much better.

Dinner guests, especially those who sat next to him or
those who did not know him very well, were naturally
somewhat nonplussed by these performances. Was Mr
Churchill ill? Was he weary of the company? Should he be
awakened and talked to?

But anyone who watched Mrs Churchill or one of her
daughters in such circumstances would get a cue. They
always let Mr Churchill be. If he were thinking of his next
speech, or working out a political problem, or remembering

an encounter with Stalin or Roosevelt, or recalling the words of a poem, why disturb him? Now and then people tried, only to wish they had not. Though Churchill was never rude, he was cool or short with anyone who interrupted or bothered him.

In fact he did not like conversational competition of any kind, except perhaps from his wife, and it was always work to break in on him or to get him to listen if he did not feel like it. Those who succeeded had to speak up loudly and clearly and present their point in their best-chosen words, for Churchill could not abide muttering, and was likely to receive a tentative murmur with an ogreish glare and a brusque, 'Eh? What was that?' As he became older, he grew increasingly hard of hearing, and often used his infirmity to devastating advantage by cupping his ear to force the loud repetition of some particularly inane remark.

His interest, even when aroused, languished quickly if he found the subject not worth his while. Once in Marrakech my wife was quietly carrying on a conversation with her neighbour when Churchill snatched at a sentence he had heard. 'Scottish Industrial Estates,' he asked, 'what are they?' My wife, well up on the subject, and pleased to be able to give the great man information he really seemed to want, turned brightly to explain. But Churchill's interest waned perceptibly after a second or two, and her fascinating exposition flickered out in mid-sentence.

Even on minor questions he was always happier when his friends agreed with him. On large matters of politics or economics, he became thoroughly annoyed if anyone slowed down his train of thought by raising objections. One evening during a vacation in the South of France Churchill began advocating the Commodity Dollar—a monetary

system whereby world currencies would be backed by commodities such as copper, coal, iron, wheat and gold. After giving a number of general reasons why it would be superior to existing monetary systems, he was then ready to listen to others, or, rather, to change the subject. But one member of the party, who considered himself an expert on money and banking, took issue with everything Churchill had said, going into the most minute and technical details to prove its impracticability. Churchill obviously neither could nor cared to follow him. Several times he interrupted with the gentle hint that he was, after all, making only a general observation. But his friend persisted. At last Churchill broke in again and this time stopped the discussion for good. 'I'm only suggesting an idea,' he said with angry finality. 'Let the experts work out the details by themselves.'

He took just as much delight in apocryphal anecdotes and epigrams attributed to him as in those that were true. 'Is that one of mine?' he would playfully ask, and would then carefully store it in his memory, to be used as his very own on a later occasion.

He was always pleased to be reminded of his own great phrases, and was particularly happy when someone corrected his misquoting of himself—something he frequently did as he grew older. 'I said at that time and I say so now,' he once rumbled, ' "I did not become His Majesty's First Minister to be present at the liquidation of the British Empire." ' 'You said "preside over," Sir,' someone put in. ' "Preside over," of course,' Churchill beamed, 'that's what I said, didn't I, and that is much better. "Preside over." ' It gratified him to realize that his words had become history and were learned by heart.

Churchill insisted on the limelight on most occasions, but he would sometimes give it up voluntarily to an exceptionally pretty and intelligent woman. Once in 1949 when Mrs Henry Luce was invited down to Chartwell for tea Churchill not only changed from his zip outfit to a sporty summer suit to honour her presence, but actually let her do most of the talking, gazing at her admiringly the while and interrupting only to pose a new question as to what she thought about this or that matter. Mrs Luce, of course, had many shrewd observations to make on politics and military defence, and Churchill was obviously fascinated by the succinct and amusing way she made her points. A great showman himself, he could appreciate the quality in others, particularly in an attractive woman.

## CHURCHILL

## THE MAN

CHURCHILL was not a man of large build. If anything he was of less than average height, but his large head, prominent turned-up nose, heavy jaw, thick neck and broad shoulders combined to give him the appearance of a bull of a man. His legs were rather small, and had to support, in addition to the heavy head and shoulders, a considerable paunch which grew bigger with age and more leisure. His hands and fingers, which were a shiny ivory white like the skin on the rest of his body, were much smaller and better shaped than one might have expected on such a rotund figure, and they were always kept in perfect condition no matter what labour they were called upon to do.

The beauty of his hands in fact meant much to Churchill, and it irked him enormously one day to read in Robert E. Sherwood's book, *Roosevelt and Hopkins*, that Harry Hopkins had once referred to his hands as 'flabby.' 'Call me fat, call me bald, even call me ugly,' said Churchill, holding up his hands and looking very wounded, 'but at least no one should say that my hands are flabby. Look, see for yourself.'

His health, except for bouts of cold, which several times

led to bronchitis and pneumonia, was unusually good. The colds generally struck three or four times a year. They were invariably accompanied by fever, and until they were gone there was no peace in the household. Churchill insisted on having his temperature taken every fifteen minutes. If no doctor was around he would try to take it himself, but he was not very good at that. Once, having insisted that a thermometer be placed at night on the table next to his bed, he was given one with the mercury missing. He was happier than usual the next morning when his doctor arrived because he had taken his temperature a number of times and had seen no signs of mercury above the fever line.

He was not only interested in all the details of his own state of health, but acted rather like a concerned mother hen about everyone else's. Anyone with him in an aeroplane was always exhorted many times to blow out his ears on taking off or landing. Once, when I was coming back from Morocco with him, we were all blowing furiously under his direction when his eye fell on one of the secretaries asleep in the front of the plane. 'Miss Sturdee,' he called; then more loudly, '*Miss Sturdee!*' Miss Sturdee awakened with a start to hear Churchill asking sternly, '*Are* you blowing out your ears?' Then quickly turning round to where his wife was sitting, he asked for about the fifth time, 'Clemmie darling, are *you* blowing?'

During the same Moroccan trip we spent a few days at Tinerhir, a little desert town beyond the Atlas Mountains. It was only about 5,000 feet above sea level, but Churchill warned us continuously about the dangers of such a high altitude. 'You must never run up the stairs,' he insisted. 'Walk up slowly and rest on the landings. Now Norman

*Frank Scherschel – Life*

PAINTING IN THE SOUTH OF FRANCE

(to his valet), you are always running up and down stairs, but you mustn't do it here. Miss Sturdee, I saw you running down a few minutes ago. You must stop that.' Wherever we went during the first day we were followed by his sonorous voice: '*Do* be careful about the stairs.'

I was always scolded if I went out into the hot sunshine without my hat. And when William Deakin, his chief assistant on the *Memoirs*, developed chicken-pox shortly before we left Marrakech, Churchill spent a good part of the day checking up on his temperature, conferring with the doctor, worrying over the possibilities of contagion, and generally looking upon the disease as his own vital concern.

Until he became very old Churchill enjoyed showing off the fine state of his own health. If he wanted a book from the shelf behind the sofa in his study, he would hop on to the sofa, reach for the book, and jump down, beaming all the while over his agility. As late as his seventy-third summer he went swimming day after day in the Mediter-ranean off the rocky shore of Lord Beaverbrook's villa near Monte Carlo. This involved walking a slippery plank twenty feet above the water between two rocks to reach the sea. The shore line itself was so rocky that Lord Beaverbrook installed a rope which bathers could use to help steady themselves when they left the water.

When he was seventy-two Churchill was operated on for a hernia which had been present for years, and although it was not causing him any discomfort his doctors advised him to have it removed while he was still young enough to undergo an operation with reasonable safety. Churchill demanded a whisky and soda half an hour after he came

C

out of the anaesthetic (and got it), and within a few weeks he was turning somersaults (his favourite water sport) in his pool at Chartwell.

After his seventy-fourth year, however, he gave up swimming on the orders of his doctors, who thought that he was less apt to get cold if he stayed out of the water. At that time, too, he had to give up riding, a sport he began as a youth at Sandhurst, and at which he became so expert that he was able to ride with the Army's best in the famous Cavalry Charge at Omdurman.

Until he was very old, Churchill liked to go for walks around his estate. (Unlike Chamberlain, Halifax, Eden and other prominent British statesmen, Churchill never went for strolls in London parks.) When the weather was fine he always wore a huge grey hat (sometimes a ten-gallon style from Texas) with feathers tucked into the band. These were added to if he discovered any pretty ones near the domains of his black swans. But he never was enough addicted to walking to do much hill climbing. His Chartwell grounds sloped rather sharply south-east into the Weald of Kent, so Churchill always arranged to have a jeep or a station wagon meet him in the valley, and from there he would drive back to the house or to some other parts of the estate.

Churchill was always doing something; there was never a time when, like most people, he simply did nothing at all. That is not to say that he always worked, for much of his time in the years before and after the war was spent playing. But he lived every minute so fully, with so much gusto, that anyone who was with him for three or four hours felt as if he had spent a day in his company. His tempo of living exhausted everyone but himself, although this effect which

he had on others was partly due to the stimulation he gave to everyone by his presence.

I remember the last days of his holidays at Marrakech in 1951. Most of the rest of us were fully exhausted by then, from a round of picnics, excursions and late parties. But the day before he left, Churchill spent most of the morning and the entire afternoon painting in the hotel's garden, was host at a dinner for the two sons of the Pasha of Marrakech in the evening and retired at about 11.30 to his studio where he continued painting until two in the morning. The next day he was off to the airport at 8.30, worked on his *Memoirs* until about an hour before we landed in Paris, and then, after a quick sleep and a whisky, got off the plane to face another few days of banquets and conferences.

He started a game of cards with the same vigour and enthusiasm that he showed in everything else he did. During the war he occasionally played bezique, but when the gin rummy craze reached England Churchill could not resist it, and when someone introduced him to Oklahoma that became the game for him. I once asked him which he liked best, gin rummy or Oklahoma. 'The degree of thrill that one gets from Oklahoma compared to gin rummy,' said Churchill, 'is in direct proportion to the effect on the nervous system of an attack of delirium tremens and a single whisky and soda.'

He hated to lose at cards but, since he was neither skilful nor lucky, he usually did. But he never paid his losses grudgingly. Though he carried no cash with him, he would make a note of his debts and send a cheque in the next mail attached to a slip of paper on which was printed, 'With the compliments of Winston S. Churchill.' Or some-

times Mrs Churchill would pay for him. In that case, he would carefully make a note of that too, and hand her an I.O.U.

In most things Churchill was orderly, but at cards he was almost fussy. He liked the table to be entirely clear except for the decks. Smoking had to be allowed because he wanted his cigar, but the place for ashtrays was on little tables nearby. That was also the place for the whiskies. If anyone inadvertently disturbed the arrangements and set his glass or ashtray down on the playing table, Churchill was visibly uncomfortable until he could find an opportunity to put things back where they belonged. Cards had to be shuffled properly and tricks stacked neatly; and he insisted on the most careful score-keeping—by someone other than himself.

He loved games, especially if they were competitive. It was he who always organized the terrifying game of 'Snapdragon' (the object of which is to pull as many raisins as possible from a bowl of blazing brandy) every Christmas for his grandchildren—and himself. But he also wanted to win, and he became childishly impatient at any obstacles that might prevent him.

In the main hall at Chequers there stood a pin-ball machine for the relaxation of tired Prime Ministers and their colleagues. Churchill took to it with enthusiasm his second week-end there after the 1951 elections. But the fact that there was only a limited number of balls to score with at one time soon irritated him beyond endurance. So he began flipping up the barrier that separated the used balls from those still in play, and, with much effort, cursing and swearing, finally tore the whole apparatus apart and thus was able to play the balls over and over again as often

as he wished. This destroyed the point of the game, according to the rules, but the system suited Churchill down to the ground and gave him a good ten minutes of complete satisfaction.

Every Sunday night, except on fine summer evenings, movies were shown at Chartwell, in a little theatre in the back of the house. Churchill derived enormous pleasure from them. He paid the strictest attention every minute and demanded absolute silence from the rest of the audience, though he reserved the right to give a running commentary if he chose and to ask questions whenever a part was not clear. He liked all sorts of pictures, but his preference seemed to run to plots with a historical background, full of sentiment and not devoid of good-looking ladies. It was not often that he saw a picture more than once, but a notable exception was *Lady Hamilton*, which he saw at least ten times, and, according to some, no less than seventeen!

One Sunday in 1949 we took five episodes of the March of Time's *Crusade in Europe*, a documentary film of World War II, down to Chartwell. Churchill loved it, as it enabled him to relive his grandest years again, and he watched it with the closest attention, tears often rolling down his cheeks and comments on the action continually on his lips. Characteristically he showed no feeling of triumph over his vanquished enemy. 'Poor fellows, poor, poor fellows,' he would say with generous pity, as towards the end he watched scenes of German prisoners-of-war huddling together in their camps. After the hour and forty minutes it took to run off the five reels, Churchill was calling for more, though it was then 11 p.m.

That evening provided a good example of Churchill's extraordinary thoughtfulness. It was the custom at Chartwell to invite everyone who lived or worked on the estate to view the movies. Among the group of twenty or thirty was an ex-German prisoner-of-war named Walter, who did odd jobs like wood-cutting and lawn-mowing, and who, from the way he responded to anything Churchill said, was obviously a devoted servant. The March of Time film was not under way more than a few minutes before it was clear that it would not evoke happy memories for a former member of the Reichswehr. Churchill rose from his seat at once, tapped Walter on the shoulder, and motioned him to leave the theatre with him. Later we learned that Churchill's object in going out was to suggest to Walter that perhaps he would prefer not to see the film that evening. Walter, however, returned to the theatre with Churchill and remained till the end.

Churchill's gusto and joy of living did not lead him to take spirits in anything like the degree to which he is generally credited. Most of his drinking—considerable to be sure—was done at meals, and there is no truth in the notion that he was an exceptionally heavy whisky drinker. He did, however, drink a good deal and, because of his unusual method of consumption, he gave the impression that he practically never stopped drinking except when he was asleep. His system was to linger over each drink for hours, and he therefore could nearly always be found with a glass no more than an arm's length away.

He usually had a drink brought to him an hour or so after breakfast. This was fairly weak, and would last until about lunch-time. At lunch he drank freely of champagne,

port and brandy. After lunch, at about 4, he would order another whisky and soda, which would almost keep him going until the time for his nap. Dinner was a repetition of lunch, and he would call for his first drink in the evening around 10 or 11, depending on when dinner ended. He would probably have a second whisky before retiring for the night at 1, 2 or 3 a.m. I never saw him pouring his own drink. He always called for his valet, and said: 'A whisky and soda, please.'

What Churchill would have done without a valet is hard to imagine. This faithful servitor woke him, brought him his breakfast, handed him his newspapers, let his dog in, took his dog out for a walk, ran the bath, dried him, took out his clothes, inserted the cuff links, helped dress him, tied his tie, handed him his hair-brushes, helped him on with his shoes, tied the laces, met him at the door when he returned from a walk or journey, took off his shoes, put on his slippers, helped him with his painting, handed him cigars, and so forth until bedtime. Each valet lasted only about a year, with the exception of one, Sawyers, a short, quiet, oldish man, who was with him during most of World War II. The job was too difficult, the hours too long (Churchill insisted on a seven-day week) to hold any-one much longer. The valets were undoubtedly devoted to Churchill although life with him, in addition to long hours, was often far from easy. He expected his valet to appear within a few seconds after he rang for him, and if there was any delay he shouted. If anything wasn't exactly right he let the valet know about it in very plain language.

From Churchill's conversation one gathered that most of his reading was done during the first half of his life while

he served in the Army or worked as a journalist. During those years he lapped up such monumental works as Gibbons's *Decline and Fall*, raced through the novels of Jane Austen and Dickens, read and reread Tennyson, Keats, Shelley, Byron, the Lake poets and many others until he had memorized a great many of their works. But after he entered politics, he no longer read voraciously. He was then too busy making history and writing it to spend much time reading, though he still probably read more books in a year than are read nowadays by the average person. Occasionally he would pick up a novel like *Gentlemen Prefer Blondes*, which years later he recalled as a delightful story. But he had no use for the run of best-selling novels or for that opiate of tired geniuses, the detective story. And though he would read marked passages of *Roosevelt and Hopkins*, and perhaps page through the war accounts of Eisenhower and Bradley, even serious books on contemporary history did not greatly tempt him.

However, when the exceptional book once caught his fancy, he would stay up all night to finish it. One of these was *1984*, the horrendous fantasy about Great Britain under totalitarianism, by the late George Orwell. And, while convalescing from his stroke of 1953, he discovered the works of Anthony Trollope, and spent many happy hours immersed in the 'political novels' of that Victorian lover of parliamentary strategy.

So great was his self-confidence that it did not bother Churchill in the slightest not to have read the book everyone was talking about or to discover that he was ignorant on a certain subject. If the book or the subject interested him he would ask to be enlightened; if it did not he would become visibly bored, change the conversation or ask that

it be changed, or he would get up and do something else.

He knew Shakespeare from start to finish, but it was not often that he went to the West End to see Laurence Olivier or John Gielgud in a Shakespearean role. He liked the theatre reasonably well, but not enough to disorganize his regular routine to the extent necessary to take in a play. He always made an exception, of course, for his daughter Sarah if she were playing in anything. Then he would put on his dinner jacket, take his seat in one of the front rows, and be all eyes and ears throughout. During intermissions he would go to her dressing-room and allow himself to be photographed with her for the London newspapers and periodicals.

One of the puzzling things about Churchill—and an aspect of his character that often astonished those who did not know him well—were the frequent gaps in his information on well-known people and subjects of general interest.

After Paul Hoffman, for instance, had been chief of the Marshall Plan organization for two years his name was still not impressed upon Churchill's mind. He had heard of him by that time, to be sure, but he still asked, 'Who's that?' as late as 1949.

When the food situation was at its worst in England after the war, and it was well known that supplies in France and certain other Continental countries were much better because they had more land for agriculture, Churchill one day turned to me and said: 'Now you go over to France a great deal: isn't it true that the people there are eating a lot better than we are here in England. Restaurants, for instance. Can't you go into one and get a very good lunch or dinner?' Churchill, who was about to discuss food supplies in a speech, was not sure of the simplest facts, although

he had spent a number of weeks the previous summer on holiday in France. He was that manner of man—oblivious to most things that did not directly concern him at the moment. But if they did become his concern, he soon learned all about them, down to the last and smallest detail.

His intense love of detail, in fact, was extraordinary in a man of such broad vision and imagination. When he returned to office in 1951 he startled and often infuriated his colleagues by interesting himself in such minor matters as the way a man's name was given in a press release, or by insisting on studying every last memorandum before action could be taken even on routine matters.

'Your trip to America was a great success, wasn't it?' I asked him shortly after his return in 1951. 'Yes, we accomplished quite a lot,' he replied. 'But,' he added sadly, 'I left many things undone in England. For instance, while I was away I could not stop them using steel in unnecessary ways. Take hutments. Steel for hutments to-day, steel for hutments to-morrow, steel for hutments of the future. I had to stop all that nonsense when I got back.'

'Should you be bothered with such detail?' I said.

'Detail?' he asked rather crossly. 'It's not just the 60,000 tons of steel for hutments that might be wasted. It's what could be done with that steel for other things that's important. A little steel here and a little steel there could mean £25,000,000 in products that we could export."

On money matters he was rather unpredictable, although he was no fool about them and always knew exactly what he was doing. All his life—until he sold his *Memoirs*—he lived to the very limit of his income, so that when he left 10 Downing Street he had to begin thinking again, at the

age of seventy, of how to make a living. It was then that he worked out the deals to sell the rights to his Secret Speeches and to some of his paintings, the earnings of which helped him to maintain Chartwell and 28 Hyde Park Gate, the town house he bought in Kensington after his defeat. When he sold the *Memoirs* his financial concerns were, of course, materially lessened, but to save taxes and to provide for his family he set up a trust into which most of the income was deposited. This trust was continually on his mind, and it was his constant fear that he might die before the five years that would make it safe from death duties had elapsed.

One day in 1950 I went down to visit him at Chartwell, and found him busily at work on a manuscript in his study.

'I've done a lot of work,' he told me happily. 'Volume Five is in good shape. It can be called a Property. And I'm getting along with Six, too.' He then jumped up and marched to the long wooden counter along the wall where a complete set of proofs was always kept. 'See,' he said. 'Eighty thousand words in the first book of Volume Five and ninety thousand in the second. If I should fall down dead to-morrow this book could carry my name.'

'But you're in the best of health,' I declared. 'You've not looked better in years.'

'I know,' he answered. 'The important thing is that I live until July 1st. By that time the trust will be five years old, and after that I can die without the Government taking most of it away in taxes. I must be careful about flying until then because I want to be sure the kids are looked after. But after July—hmmm—then I can fly like hell. I'm getting £35,000 out of Volume Five. That's plenty for me, but nothing of that will be left for the trust.

Still the trust has had five whacks at the book already. Not so bad.'

In many ways Churchill was one of the most extravagant of men. Several years after the war he spent £5,000 to build a small new reservoir at Chartwell because he was not satisfied with the water flow; less than a month later he came to the conclusion that the reservoir was not necessary at all.

At other times he could be extremely cautious. When a storm struck Kent and caused havoc among his trees Churchill spent a morning negotiating a fee of £50 to be paid to a local tree doctor for patching up some of the worst damage near the house. In the weeks that followed Churchill himself spent many mornings sawing up limbs that had been blown down.

In 1956 he turned down an offer of $25,000 for the reproduction rights to twelve of his paintings, which comprised only a very small part of his vast collection. 'I sometimes give them away, but I never sell them,' he said. When I reminded him that ten years earlier he had sold *Life* Magazine some reproduction rights, he chuckled: 'Things were different then. I needed the money. Now I don't. If I did, I would not hesitate for a minute.'

Churchill adored gambling, and it was Mrs Churchill's constant worry that he would squander more money at the gaming tables than the family finances could stand. On his return one year from a visit to France as guest of several of his American publishers he asked me to come and see him immediately as there was something on his mind. 'I have a confession to make,' he said, 'and I don't know what I can do about the situation that has been created.' He then told how he had used some of the vacation funds to buy a

suit in Monte Carlo. 'I could, of course, pay you back in sterling, but that's against the law,' he said. After a pause he continued: 'And that isn't all. I went to the casino one or two nights, and ended up a little behind. I did very well at first, but then my luck changed. What *am* I to do about it?'

By normal standards Churchill was rather a vain man. He was by no means unaware of the fact that he possessed the most effective voice of any public figure of his time, and that he was a master of the English language. It gave him supreme enjoyment to read aloud to one or two friends something he had written, or, if that was inconvenient, to have someone around reading in silence a new chapter from his book. He thrived on praise and appreciation, and when they were not forthcoming he was miserable. He carefully noted whether his speeches and doings made front page news or not.

For though he always professed a disgust for the press generally, and for press reporters in particular ('Of course you can't believe anything you read in the papers,' was one of his frequent comments), he took his newspapers very seriously and was always anxious to read the latest reports on his own or his Party's activities. One of my regular duties, never laid down in so many words but a strict one nevertheless, was to bring him all the early editions of the evening papers when I visited Chartwell of an afternoon. If I forgot, Churchill was visibly disappointed. It fretted him to have to wait even that extra hour or so until the usual time of their arrival.

If the newspapers attacked him, he felt it keenly. He would worry over the ill-starred passage for hours, and

keep referring to it in conversation, as if hoping for re-
assurance from those around him that he was not such a
bad fellow after all.

I remember lunching with him one day at 10 Downing
Street, when he was brooding about an *Economist* editorial
that had criticized him for lack of vigour and imagination
in attacking the economic crisis. 'What's this man Crowther
like?' he suddenly boomed forth in the middle of some
desultory table-talk. 'Here he is telling me I'm not govern-
ing well. How can he sit back in his office and know just
what a government should or should not do? Well, I'd just
like him to try running the country, for a day or two, that's
all. It isn't as easy as he thinks. I'm going to meet him
sometime soon, and I'll tell him so.'

It was probably hurt vanity and pride which partly
accounted for his utter dejection after his defeat in the
1945 election, which perhaps pained him as much as anything did in his lifetime. The thought of defeat so soon
after the end of the war had never crossed his mind, and
for months he was hardly able to comprehend the actual
fact of it. 'No sooner was our peril over than they turned
me out,' he muttered sadly to me many weeks later.

He always wanted to have his own way, and on the rare
occasions when he failed to get it he was cross and unhappy.
It was not easy to take up a problem with him of any kind,
and it was almost impossible to get him to change his mind
about a thing. Nothing was so difficult as to talk to
Churchill on the telephone about any serious subject. He
had a devastating way of failing to hear any objections to
his own scheme or any points the person might be making
at the other end of the line—unless he wanted to.

In 1948 I was invited to visit Churchill during his

holidays at Aix-en-Provence. His assistant, William Deakin, and I had arranged to go together and make something of an excursion out of it by driving slowly down through France in Deakin's ancient Rolls. The day was set, the car's papers had been put in order, and we had our channel steamer tickets when, several days before we proposed to set out, Deakin got a telephone call from Churchill at Aix.

The conversation went something like this:

Churchill: 'Bill, I am very hard pressed. I want you to come down right away. Take to-morrow's plane and I'll have a car meet you at the airport.'

Deakin: 'I'm so sorry, Sir, but I can't possibly get away that early. I have a lot of work to wind up here at Oxford and can't leave for at least four days. Walter Graebner and I are planning to drive down then if that's all right with you.'

Churchill: 'What's that you say? I can't hear you. I need you down here very much. Get on the plane as fast as you can. We'll arrange everything from this end.'

Deakin: 'But, Sir, I said I can't possibly do it. There is work I must finish up here first.'

Churchill: 'This connection is very bad. I can't hear a word you say. We'll see you to-morrow then, Good-bye.'

Needless to say, Deakin left immediately, and I had to follow by train.

# CHAPTER FOUR

## CHURCHILL'S
## DAY

I ONCE marvelled to Churchill at the perfect way he organized his work, and offered this as an explanation for his fantastic ability to accomplish so much each day. 'Not at all,' he said, 'my work is highly organized so that I can have more time for *leisure*.'

Churchill's day began at 8, no matter when he went to bed. At that hour all the London daily newspapers were brought in, including the Communist *Daily Worker*, which Churchill considered accurate and enlightening on non-political subjects. He was also a steady reader of the *Manchester Guardian* ('the best newspaper in the world'), greatly respected the *Christian Science Monitor*, and every week he had a good look at *The Economist*. His reading took him the better part of an hour as he sat in bed, propped up with pillows, eating a good solid breakfast of fruit, eggs, meat or fish, toast and coffee.

Once I saw him at 10 Downing Street during a newspaper reading session. The stack of papers next to him in his enormous bed was especially large that morning as he had just returned by overnight train from Glasgow, where he had made an important political speech, and he was anxious to know how the press treated him. He picked up

*Philippe Halsman – Life*

WITH RUFUS, OVERLOOKING THE CHARTWELL PONDS

one paper after another, glanced at it quickly to measure the size of the headline, then flung it aside. Every few minutes he would ring for a secretary to demand a later edition. 'These all went to press *before* I spoke,' he growled. 'I want to know what they said *afterwards*.'

He remained in bed all morning as a rule. Only special circumstances, such as a Cabinet crisis, or a warm and sunny day at Chartwell, could induce him to rise before lunch. He liked having his feet up, and his mind worked well and quickly in bed. It was easy for him to stay in bed and work because near at hand was everything that anyone could want in an office. The big double bed provided plenty of space on both sides for papers, books, and so on. Work in actual progress was done on a short-legged mahogany tray about $30 \times 18$ inches which fitted snugly over his torso. For greater comfort the tray was fitted with a set of small rubber pads on which he could rest his elbows. Within easy reach of his bed, whether at Chartwell, Hyde Park Gate or 10 Downing Street, stood a narrow table with two telephones—a direct line to his secretaries' office downstairs, and an outside connection; a gold case of cigars, one of which he was always smoking or at least holding; a tall white candle, always aglow, for lighting and relighting the cigars; a large gold pocket watch; strips of brown paper specially made by Cartier's to wrap round his cigars and so prevent the juice from running down; a gold ball-point pen and many pencils; a pink-coloured, mild form of sleeping pill, called Soneryl, which many London doctors were then prescribing; a strong type of aspirin, called Veganin, which he sometimes took in the mornings to stop severe headaches; a huge diary about a foot square noting his engagements.

D

Churchill never went to see anybody on business unless protocol (such as that applying to the Royal Family) dictated that he should. People always came to see him—another reason why he could get so much work done, and have so much time for leisure. And if the appointment was at any time before 12.30, Churchill remained in bed, though he was, of course, shaved by the time anyone arrived.

The visitor was welcomed with the usual broad beam and extended hand, asked to sit down in a comfortable armchair and invited to 'have a whisky and soda—or would you like port better?' Churchill also took the opportunity of ordering a whisky and soda for himself, if he did not already have one.

Every important appointment was meticulously prepared for in advance by the secretarial staff. On a single sheet of paper were typed the points to be discussed, and fastened to the sheet by a string through punch holes were any documents or correspondence relating to the matter. Unless a subject was of extraordinary urgency, Churchill did not rush to the point at once, or seem particularly anxious to get down to business at all. Sometimes he would talk for fifteen or twenty minutes before finally saying: 'Have we any business to take up?'

He would never make a quick decision, and any attempt to hurry him was met with a scowl or a growl. It did not trouble him at all to sit silently for ten minutes thinking over a point, even with a visitor in the room. Minor problems concerned with the running of his estate were often no more hastily dealt with than a tricky diplomatic question. He welcomed advice, 'but,' he once said, 'of course, I don't have to follow it.'

Churchill valued his time so highly that even the barber came once a week to his bedroom to cut his hair in the few stray moments between bath and lunch. 'I'll give you five minutes and no more,' Churchill usually quipped on these occasions. The cutting of his hair was nothing private. 'Oh, don't go,' Churchill would tell his visitor, 'we can go on talking quite happily.'

There was usually slight pandemonium as the lunch hour approached and Churchill continued working in his bedroom. Mrs Churchill sometimes tried to hurry him along by looking in and saying: 'Come, Winston, it's a quarter to one and you must be downstairs when Count Sforza gets here.' These entreaties of Mrs Churchill were greeted with a warm grin, and Churchill always agreed but never hurried. Most of the time, however, he did reach the drawing-room at least by the time those guests who were not well known to the family arrived. It was a matter of pride with him that he could leave his bed and be downstairs, bathed and dressed, in seven minutes. 'I never take more than three minutes to bathe and four—at the most five—to dress,' he often said. It was four minutes when he wore his zip suit and five on the occasions when he wore ordinary clothes.

Lunch at 10 Downing Street or at Hyde Park Gate never lasted less than an hour and a half, even when Parliament was in session, while at Chequers or Chartwell, if guests were present, it often went on for nearly three hours. In the next hour, if Churchill was in the country, he got his main exercise of the day by taking a walk with one or more of his guests. These walks, however, were not just aimless meanderings through the gardens; the time was spent examining the water levels in the various reservoirs,

feeding the fish, throwing a ball for Rufie to chase, and perhaps declaiming on the state of the world.

Churchill never bothered with the English rite of afternoon tea. Even when guests had stayed over from lunch, he usually sent them off to the dining-room with Mrs Churchill, and dropped in himself only at the very end of the meal. Tea at Chartwell in any event was somewhat of a nursery affair, and more often than not consisted of assorted grandchildren in high chairs, a bevy of nannies, the usual number of dogs and only one or two stray adults.

When Churchill did turn up it was usually with a whisky and soda in hand and a cigar in his mouth. He would arrange himself in a comfortable chair and watch the proceedings from the sidelines. Baby talk was not one of his strong points, and since he probably felt that his customary prose would be lost on his audience, he would limit his communication at these tea parties to a few broad smiles for the children and one or two cheerful phrases for the nannies.

At the end of the afternoon he sometimes asked a person to come and see him for a business talk over a drink. When this happened it was even more leisurely than a morning bedside session, because he seldom had any more appointments before dinner and because the wines of lunch had relaxed him to the point where he was less aware of the time. He also took a half hour around six o'clock to scan the afternoon papers, see a movie, read any letters his secretary thought would interest him, and read and sign his own letters and memos. After that he would sleep for an hour or two.

About ten minutes before dinner his valet would wake him and he would quickly shave, bathe and dress. By the

time he appeared his guests were well into their second sherry, ready to be led into dinner as soon as Churchill had finished his tomato juice.

Around 10.30 or 11, well-fed, rested, happy and free of his guests, Churchill settled down to two or three hours of hard, concentrated work, during which he accomplished more than in any other period. If he was alone he usually got into bed to work, with a secretary seated nearby; if others were helping him he sat with them around the table. His valet was always on call to keep him (and, if necessary, his helpers) amply supplied with drink and tobacco. At least one secretary was available at all times to take dictation and to type a draft for immediate perusal. It was during these late evening and early morning sessions that Churchill composed the first drafts of many of his great speeches and wrote some of the finest chapters of his books. Often the last thing he did at night when in London was to scan the first edition of the *Daily Express* which his great and good friend Lord Beaverbrook rushed to him by dispatch-rider. Sometimes, if big news was being made, he would get on the telephone and impatiently quiz a sleepy night editor about headlines and lead stories. Churchill seldom got to bed before 2 a.m.

Late in life Churchill for a while considered dispensing with his team of secretaries, at least for night work, and using machinery to record his thoughts. He allowed the SoundScriber Company of America to install, free of charge, the most advanced machine its engineers could design, equipped with microphones that could pick up his voice wherever he was—whether in his bed, his bath or his study. It went for hours without requiring new discs and it started and stopped from the action of the sound waves.

Churchill was fascinated by the wonderful equipment, and derived a good deal of pleasure from trying it out. But he never thought seriously of using it. 'I'm too old for that kind of thing,' he said. 'I think I'll go on using secretaries as long as I can afford them. Anyway, I rather like having them around when I work.'

The installation of the SoundScriber, however, did give Mr Churchill a chance to give in his own words his recipe for combining a full working day with the good life. I was with the head of the SoundScriber Company, a Mr Gfroerer, when he went down to Chartwell to supervise the installation of the machine, and listened in on the following conversation:

Churchill: 'What is your day in America like (looking Mr Gfroerer straight in the eye)? What time do you get to your office and when do you stop working?'

Gfroerer: 'I'm at my desk every morning at 8 and leave at 5.30. At noon I have a short break for lunch. We do that five days a week, and sometimes I go around to the office Saturday mornings to read the mail.'

Churchill: 'My dear man, you don't mean it. That is the most perfect prescription for a short life that I've ever heard.'

Mr Gfroerer, a little frightened and somewhat staggered by Churchill's sudden probing into his private life, then confessed that his wife also did not approve of his hours at all, and would certainly be delighted to hear the views of Mr Churchill.

Gfroerer: 'Mrs Gfroerer hates to get up at 6.45 and have breakfast so early. Then she doesn't see me until 6 in

the evening. We have dinner early, and by 10 I'm so
tired that I fall into bed and am asleep in two minutes.
I know I've got to slow down. That's what Mrs
Gfroerer is always telling me.'

Churchill: 'You must sleep some time between lunch and
dinner, and no half-way measures. Take off your
clothes and get into bed. That's what I always do.
Don't think you will be doing less work because you sleep
during the day. That's a foolish notion held by people
who have no imagination. You will be able to accomplish more. You get two days in one—well, at least
one and a half, I'm sure. When the war started, I *had*
to sleep during the day because that was the only way
I could cope with my responsibilities. Later, when I
became Prime Minister, my burdens were, of course,
even greater. Often I was obliged to work far into the
night. I had to see reports, take decisions and issue
instructions that could not wait until the next day.
And at night I'd also dictate minutes requesting
information which my staff could assemble for me in
the morning—and place before me when I woke up.'

Churchill relighted his cigar, poured himself a little
more brandy, passed the bottle, and continued:

'But a man should sleep during the day for another
reason. Sleep enables you to be at your best in the
evening when you join your wife, family and friends
for dinner. That is the time to be at your best—a good
dinner, with good wines (champagne is *very* good)
then some brandy—that is the great moment of the
day. Man is ruler then—perhaps only for fifteen
minutes, but for that time at least he is master—and

the ladies must not leave the table too soon.'

Gfroerer: 'I must slow down. My wife has been telling me that for years, but something is always happening at the office. Mrs Gfroerer will agree with everything you've said when I tell her.'

Churchill: 'Do you always get up for breakfast?'

Gfroerer: 'But, of course.'

Churchill: 'Your wife, too?'

Gfroerer: 'Why, yes.'

Churchill: 'My, my! My wife and I tried two or three times in the last forty years to have breakfast together, but it didn't work. Breakfast should be had in bed, alone. Not downstairs, after one has dressed.' His eyes twinkling, Churchill added: 'I don't think our married life would have been nearly so happy if we both had dressed and come down for breakfast all these years.'

Toward the end of his life, Churchill's longing for a good sleep became almost an obsession, and when he failed to get one, he acted a little as if he had been cheated. One summer's day at Chartwell, when he told me rather grumpily that he had awakened two mornings in succession at six, I asked him whether he was still taking sleeping pills. 'One every night for the last 10 years,' he said proudly. Since it was nearly time for his afternoon nap, I ventured the suggestion that he have a pill then and there, adding that he was only taking a half-dose anyway. Churchill quickly sent for his pills, and rather revengefully popped one into his mouth. About 20 minutes later he happily announced that he was off to bed.

# CHAPTER FIVE

# CHURCHILL

# AT THE TABLE

'My tastes are simple, I like only the best,' Winston Churchill once remarked, and choice food and drink were high on the list of life's best things for him. Like the lusty Elizabethan he was at heart, he was an excellent trencherman, and approached the two main meals of the day with both enthusiasm and respect. It was not, however, solely the delights of eating and drinking that made lunch and dinner the high points of his day. It was also the fact that these two occasions were often the only times for relaxation in a long and busy day, the only times when he could have his family and friends around him in carefree and informal conviviality. Therefore, he made the most of them.

He never spent much time serving his guests drinks before lunch or dinner. It was a special occasion indeed when cocktails were made, and even when they were produced, Mr Churchill rarely took one. His average was probably two a year—a fact often not taken into account by those who believe that Churchill was a heavy drinker. As a rule only sherry and tomato juice were served before meals, and Churchill always took tomato juice. After one glass—at the most two—was drunk, Churchill suggested

going into the dining-room.

There was never any formality at meals. More often than not Rufie would be in the room, lying down either at his master's feet or in a special chair beside him; and Churchill would act like all indulgent masters everywhere, slipping him a piece of food, throwing a ball for him in between courses, or breaking off a conversation to pet him or call him 'my darling Rufie.'

Sometimes his daughter, Mary Soames, would bring one or both of her two dogs, a Labrador retriever and a toy poodle, over for a meal, and the dining-room would take on the aspect of a jolly menagerie. And once my black poodle puppy, Pol Roger, was there as well, with rather alarming consequences. For Rufie, who had been an exemplary host while we were all in the drawing-room, became wildly jealous as soon as Pol began to compete for the master's attention—and food. Two raucous fights ensued, each time subdued only by Churchill throwing his table-napkin over Rufie's head and scolding him in his best rhetorical style. In almost any other house I might have been discomfited at having introduced such an obvious interloper, but at Chartwell the easy, home-like atmosphere was so pervasive that I do not believe it occurred to me to make even a perfunctory apology.

I remember one incident which shows perhaps as well as anything the cosy family quality of the Churchill *ménage*. I and several other guests were dining quietly at Chartwell, when suddenly Mrs Churchill, usually the soul of tact and the keenest supporter of her husband, began criticizing Volume III of the *Memoirs*, saying it was too full of minutes and memos and was all rather dull. Mr Churchill reddened with anger—rather naturally so, since

in actual fact he had just been defending his work against the same criticisms from his publishers, myself included. He began barking out his irritation at his 'Clemmie,' and for a while the atmosphere grew tense and strained. But not for long. 'Now, Winston dear, you really cannot talk to me that way,' broke in Mrs Churchill, and—with a humorous pretence at anger—flung her large dinner-napkin across the table at her irate spouse. Peace was immediately restored, amid loud laughter, the loudest of all coming from Mr Churchill; and Mrs Churchill, like the wise general she was, instantly took advantage of the prevailing good humour to marshall her ladies around her and sweep from the room.

Nor was there any formality with the servants who waited at the table. Churchill talked to them, scolded them, gave them orders throughout the entire meal. It was, 'John, are you sure this bottle is properly chilled?' or 'John, where did we get these oysters? They aren't very good,' or 'Doris, *don't* take away the butter plates. We want to save them for our *pâté.*' Not for Churchill, the upper-class English convention that table servants are invisible and can only be communicated with by surreptitious gestures and low mutterings.

At the very beginning of the meal, almost before anyone had pulled his chair in, a bottle of well-chilled champagne would be brought in and placed in front of Mr Churchill. It has been said that a guest could feel particularly honoured or welcome if champagne was served, and some-what snubbed if the wine were anything else. There can be little truth in this, because for years Churchill served only champagne in his house for lunch and dinner unless, through oversight, the champagne cellar happened to be

empty. His favourite brand was Pol Roger 1928, cases of which arrived from time to time at Chartwell and Hyde Park Gate from the Pol Roger family in France, some of whom were friends of the Churchills. When there were six or eight present at a meal—the Churchills seldom entertained large numbers except on very formal occasions—a magnum-sized bottle was sometimes used, and Churchill always poured for everyone within reach. Then he would pass the bottle along and ask the others to help themselves. He took great care to see that the bottle was always passed to the left. Passing to the right was bad luck, and Churchill was very superstitious. (To sit down thirteen to table, for instance, would have been an abomination to him.) The minute a bottle was empty he would ring for another, and no glass was allowed to be empty from the beginning of the meal to the end.

I never learned whether Churchill paid for the thousands of bottles of champagne he and his friends drank, or whether most of them were gifts from the Pol Rogers. But if Churchill was indebted he more than made repayment by naming one of his best race-horses Pol Roger.

Though Churchill loved food and always eagerly looked forward to a meal, his table, while far better than the English average, was not sumptuous. The first course was very likely to be an egg dish, smoked salmon or hors d'œuvres, perhaps only sardines. The main course was often fowl, rarely a roast, with potatoes, vegetables and salad. The dessert or sweet was the important course for Mr Churchill. A baked tart, submerged in thick cream from his own cows, suited him fine. This was followed by cheese, with port. Churchill was especially fond of Stilton, which he enjoyed scooping out of its cylindrical form.

Though all the Stilton was exported from England during the first four post-war years, Churchill had enough thoughtful friends in the United States to keep him supplied most of the time. 'Stilton and port,' he announced one day, as these delicacies were being placed upon the table, 'are like man and wife. They should never be separated. "Whom God has joined together, let no man put asunder." No—nor woman either.'

If any dish did not meet with Churchill's whole-hearted approval, he was loud in his complaints or in suggestions for its improvement. Once at Chartwell, he found the oysters not quite to his liking. He sampled a few, grunting and expostulating as each one went down, then summarily dismissed the offending dish, and that of each of his guests as well. At Chequers on another occasion, a rather mediocre mince tart was brought in for dessert. When Mr Churchill saw it, he called for some brandy. 'Everybody,' he said firmly, 'must pour some brandy on the plum pudding. It has not been brought in flaming, so we shall have to do the next best thing.' A bottle of cognac was immediately produced, and everybody did as directed, from the Duchess of Marlborough to the eminent scientist Lord Cherwell, a confirmed vegetarian and teetotaller.

A bottle of brandy, usually full, was placed on the table when coffee was served. After pouring himself about three-quarters of an inch in a brandy glass he passed the bottle along and implored everyone to help himself. A refusal was met with another request. Only women were excepted, though once while on holiday at Marrakech Churchill managed to persuade Lady Moran, the wife of his physician, to drink a small portion every evening at dinner. Churchill advocated it on grounds of health.

At this point in the meal the principles of teetotal Lord Cherwell, if he were present, always fared as badly as they had with the plum pudding. 'The professor must have his 3 c.c.s,' Churchill would say, beaming broadly at his own joke. The old scientist would make a few attempts at demurring, but his diffident objections were never proof against Churchill's ebullience. The 3 c.c.s were poured, and sipped gingerly during the many rounds the brandy bottle made among the others.

With brandy came the cigars and again every man was urged to take one. He could not understand why anyone ever preferred cigarettes, which Churchill, to my knowledge, never smoked, to cigars. 'Man hasn't lived until he has acquired the habit of smoking cigars. These are so mild, too. Try one,' he would beseech, 'and tell me if you've ever smoked anything so mild before.' Churchill got his cigars from an admiring Cuban grower who yearly put aside enough of his best leaves to maintain the stocks at Chartwell and Hyde Park Gate. Each one had 'Winston Churchill' printed on the band. Between himself and his friends the daily consumption probably ran to eighteen, though in the latter years of his life Churchill gave in to his doctor's demands that he cut down.

Brandy and cigar time was, next to going to sleep, the greatest bliss of the day. He loved it, and it was the desire to have others share in his own happiness that no doubt caused him to urge his friends so strongly to join him in his drinking and smoking. It was during this half-hour, hour or even two-hour period that Churchill was at his best. It was his hour, his show, and he was the dominating figure. This was story- and joke-telling time; the time for song, poems, reminiscences, laughter and prophecies; the time

to talk about politics, to give advice, to drink toasts and to be sentimental. His moods rose and fell like waves. If something reminded him of the past glory of England his eyes filled with tears as he talked about it. If he described one of his adventures in the Boer War he was probably roaring with laughter the next minute.

Meanwhile more and more brandy was poured. There have been times when a party of five or six nearly finished a full bottle before rising from luncheon or dinner. The only effect ever noticeable on Churchill besides an uplift in spirits was a tendency towards drowsiness. Towards the end of a brandy-cigar session—one of which, I remember, lasted after lunch till 4.22—he sometimes looked as if he could not stay awake for another minute. But once up and around the house or walking in his garden, he would quickly revive and be ready for the rest of the day's activities.

# CHAPTER SIX

# CHURCHILL

# AT WORK

A POPULAR misconception concerning Winston Churchill is that speech-making and writing came easily to him. 'How could it have been otherwise?' people ask. *The Life of Marlborough* in six volumes; *The World Crisis* in four or five volumes; millions of words of his *Memoirs;* and throughout the war, speeches in the House of Commons and over the radio which will be quoted for many years to come; after the war, Fulton, Massachusetts Institute of Technology, and scores of memorable performances in Parliament both as the Leader of the Opposition and as Prime Minister again. Only a man with an incredibly facile pen and an extraordinary ability to think on his feet, it is usually said, could have produced such masterpieces.

But the truth is that, although he had unusual gifts for composition and for turning a phrase, he worked to reach perfection as probably few people in his time ever did. He was well aware of his extraordinary command of the English language, and so, like a beautiful woman who is always meticulously groomed, he went to a great deal of time and trouble preparing and polishing his speeches. One day, after he had made a particularly stirring and

brilliant address in Parliament, I asked him a question that had long been on my mind. 'How is it possible that after those short pauses during your speeches you always, without fail, come through with just the right word or some magnificent phrase?' Churchill replied: 'I'll tell you a secret, but keep it under your hat. Those pauses are just part of my trade. I always—well, most of the time—know exactly what I am going to say, but I make believe, by hesitating a little, that a word or phrase has just come to me. I think the effect is improved.'

He took such delight in an apt phrase or a nicely-turned retort that even the ephemeral wit of Parliamentary back-chat caused him concern. One December day during a heated debate a Labour member referred to him as a goose, and Churchill replied, adequately enough but not very brilliantly, 'I do not in the least mind being called a goose. I have been called worse things than that.' The next day we lunched with him and discussed the exchange. 'I thought afterwards of what I should have replied,' said Churchill. 'What a pity I did not think of it at the time. I should have said, "I do not object to being called a goose—not even at Christmas-time!" '

No man to waste a good idea, he managed to serve it up that very afternoon in a different guise. Referring to a Labour member's promise to eat his hat if his party had not won many by-elections by the end of the year, Churchill added happily, 'I do not think such an un-palatable ordeal is needed at a time when the Christmas season is upon us, and there will be other things to eat.'

Because he considered himself inexpert at impromptu speeches he tried never to be trapped into making one, and when he was caught he always spoke briefly and simply.

E

His son, Randolph, is actually a better extemporaneous speaker than his father was, and it has been said by friends of the family that Churchill's admiration for his son's skill in this respect was mingled with a touch of envy.

Each major speech was a worrying challenge to him. About five days before it was to be delivered he would become slightly fretful and complain about being 'hard pressed.' Work then began. 'I always need four or five days to write an important speech,' he often said. Facts, figures and memoranda were brought to him to help him understand and document his case. He spent a lot of time thinking in silence, at meals, in bed or during a walk. Now and then he would reach for a pencil to make a note on the nearest piece of paper of a phrase, word or idea that he wanted to incorporate.

As the speech took shape in his mind he would often try out parts of it on his friends. Some weeks before he left England for Fulton, Missouri, to make the historic address there, I was with him in a small cottage at Chartwell which he then used as a studio. It was a lazy wintry afternoon, and Churchill was apparently thinking of nothing but his paintings, which completely covered the four walls of the cottage. For an hour or so we looked at them and discussed them, then suddenly, without warning, he began an impassioned plea for a United States of Europe. 'What do you think of that?' said Churchill. 'Would something along those lines be suitable for my speech in America?'

I was a little surprised later to note that the Fulton speech contained no reference whatever to the United States of Europe. He had thought of something else to talk about. But the subject was saved for an engagement in

Zurich, and on that occasion he used phrases very similar
to those he tried out months before in his studio.

The actual composition of a speech took many long,
strenuous hours. He never sat down to write or type a line
of the original draft. Every word was dictated to one of his
secretaries, who operated in relays. Sometimes he worked
in bed, sometimes in his study, marching up and down the
room as he talked. Pauses, while he searched for the exact
word he wanted, often lasted for five or ten minutes, and
it was his habit to repeat over and over to himself, in an
almost inaudible voice, the last few words of a sentence
before going on to the next one. In this way he developed
the magnificent flow and sweep of his pronouncements.

The minute he stopped dictating, the secretary would
go to her office and type out the draft on a plain white
piece of paper, leaving wide margins and plenty of room
between the lines. This was done for each period of dictation, even if no more than fifty or a hundred words had
been added, for Churchill liked to see everything down on
paper. He would then correct, polish, add or scrap, and
return the draft to the secretarial staff for retyping. Then
would come more bouts of dictation. In this way he built
up the whole.

He was never entirely satisfied with a speech, and continued to work on it right up till the time of delivery. Often
he was still revising and polishing an hour or so before he
was due to go on the air or to stand up in Parliament.

When the plans were being made for his M.I.T. address,
pressing invitations reached Chartwell from Boston asking
him to a reception and/or dinner before the speech.
I cannot do that,' said Churchill. 'They are so kind, but I
am an old man. I will be in bed up to an hour before I

speak, resting and working on the speech. Some people perhaps can do otherwise, but not me.'

When he made radio broadcasts he usually insisted on being alone in the room with one or two technicians. But on one occasion at Chartwell he asked me to sit in front of him while he spoke. After a family dinner, we went down to a little library-trophy room on the ground floor and made ourselves comfortable with whiskies and sodas.

Churchill just had time, before going on the air, to check the position of the microphone, leaf through his manuscript, light a tall candle so that, if necessary, he could relight his cigar without noisily scratching matches, and place his large gold pocket-type watch on the table at his right. Exactly twenty-five minutes later Churchill finished his talk to the nation, then returned with me to rejoin the dinner party which, incidentally, did not seem to be extraordinarily impressed by the great man's effort for the evening.

Churchill prided himself on his ability to time his broadcasts and speeches to the second. Accordingly, it was his habit to check his watch every minute or so to see how he was doing. If the time seemed to be rushing away he would speed up his talk, and if he had time to spare he would either slow down or try to enlarge on a point or two. This strict attention to timing explains the unusually long pauses which sometimes occurred in his speeches, pauses which obviously had no rhetorical function. During them Churchill was no doubt quietly looking at his watch and calculating.

Every week he received at least one or two invitations to make a speech somewhere. Most of them came from the United States, and were often accompanied by the offer of

an extremely tempting fee ranging anywhere from $10,000 to $50,000. 'I could spend all my remaining years,' Churchill once said, 'making speeches and travelling around the world accepting honours that kind people wish to bestow on me.'

Churchill spent far less time in finding the right phrase or the proper simile when working on his books than when preparing his speeches. The *Memoirs* seemed to gallop along, and indeed many sections suffered from his obvious desire to get them finished as soon as possible. Time was of the essence, not only because of his many other important activities, but because his publishers were always needling him for new instalments. Accordingly, much of the *Memoirs* was composed in a rush, often, indeed, dictated in the car as Churchill drove from Chartwell to some political engagement in London. 'I got eight hundred words done to-day, going up to London and back,' he once said proudly.

Of course, the words he dictated in his car or rattled off in the few minutes between his bath and a luncheon appointment were never his final phrases. Though not as scrupulously polished as his speeches, the manuscripts for his books were still subject to careful scrutiny and revision as first the typed copies and then the galley proofs in the various stages were brought to him for editing. Many of the best passages of the *Memoirs* were added almost on the final proof, when Churchill put the whole force of his fine concentration to work on the pages before him.

That, indeed, was his formula for writing: 'I write a book,' he once told me, 'the way they built the Canadian Pacific Railway. First I lay the track from coast to coast, and after that I put in all the stations.'

He observed this formula right up to the end. Not long after his severe stroke the summer the Queen was crowned, he invited me to lunch at Chartwell with two members of his writing staff to rework and improve the chapter on the great Battle of Leyte Gulf which broke Japan's sea power. Work began at the luncheon table after the second bottle of champagne was emptied and cigars were lighted. 'Now let's get down to it,' Churchill said. We were still sitting there at a quarter to five, Churchill having gone over every word in the manuscript to make sure that he understood the full story of the battle and that he had related it clearly and in his best words. In the years that I knew him his mind was never sharper than on that grey August afternoon in 1953.

# CHAPTER SEVEN

## *CHURCHILL*

## *AT PLAY*

CHURCHILL loved every square inch of the British Isles but, like so many Englishmen, when it came to a vacation he had a passion for going abroad. After the war he was, of course, subject to the severe travel restrictions imposed by the Labour Government to conserve foreign exchange. 'Beastly business,' he called the restrictions. 'Why do they [the Labour Government] want to keep people locked up in these islands all the time!' (When Churchill returned to power in 1951 he learned more about the need for the restrictions, and immediately reduced the travel allowance even further.)

Between the end of the war and his second Prime Ministership, however, Churchill did manage, through the help of his American publishers, to take one or two long holidays abroad every year, and he made the most of them. Preparations began many months in advance. First, globes and atlases were examined to choose the suitable region. The only lands that qualified were those that abounded in sunshine and bright colours, as above all Churchill wanted to paint in the sun. But the vacation spot could not be too hot or too cold. Once, after having satisfied himself that Lake Garda in Italy would be perfect for a month, he

moved on after a week because he thought it was too hot. Another time, he went from Annecy to Venice because the French Alps were too cold.

Whenever it became known that Churchill was planning a holiday, suggestions, and often invitations, reached him from many quarters. The French Ambassador was always ready with the name of a good hotel in Aix-en-Provence or on the Basque coast, while the Spanish Tourist Office sent along tantalizing descriptions of Majorca and the Costa Brava. Lord Beaverbrook offered his spacious villa on the French Riviera whenever Churchill felt like going, and there was always an American admirer who had a place in Florida to put at his disposal. Every idea was carefully studied and discussed, but most times, before a final decision was taken, the London manager of Thomas Cook & Sons, the travel agents, was called in for advice.

A recurring problem was to find a hotel big enough, or with enough rooms available, to hold the entire party. And did the windows of all the principal rooms face on to the water? Were there enough telephones? Where was the nearest airport? Could Mr Churchill avoid all public engagements? Would there be adequate local police protection? Shortly before the Egyptian riots in 1951 Churchill had to abandon carefully-laid plans for a cruise along the Nile because the British Ambassador in Cairo was not able to get satisfactory assurances from King Farouk that adequate protection would be given.

Hotels turned themselves inside out to make Churchill comfortable. The one on Lake Garda, where he stayed only a week, spent millions of lire remodelling an entire wing, replacing much of the furniture, and installing a new motor in a lift that had broken down some years before.

Large stocks of Scotch whisky, red and white port and brandy were brought in (Churchill usually took his own cigars and champagne), and a fleet of automobiles was reserved for the duration of the stay.

No matter how far he went, whether by rail or air, Churchill took with him all the equipment for an office, other than tables and chairs. Nothing was left to chance: he wanted an office functioning within an hour or two after his arrival. Crates and black dispatch boxes were filled with typewriters, paper clips, pencils, ink, paper, paste, scissors, pins, envelopes, sealing-wax, seals and string. The office was always installed near the middle of the Churchill wing, since it functioned as the nerve centre for the entire party. All mail, for example, was delivered to the office, not to the rooms of any individuals. If anyone wanted to find out who was coming to dinner he inquired at the office. All plans for the day were issued through the office. The management of this vital part of the holiday operation was entrusted to two secretaries from the London staff, one of whom was available whenever Churchill called between 8 a.m. and 2 a.m.

Equally important was the installation on arrival of a studio where Churchill could paint when inclement weather kept him indoors, and where he could display his works in various stages of completion as the holiday moved along. One large, well-lighted room was set aside for this, and the equipment brought from England included about fifteen frames, several dozen canvases, six or eight easels, and three or four powerful lamps.

There were always about a dozen people in the Churchill entourage. Two were Scotland Yard detectives, who worked twelve-hour shifts each so that Churchill was never

left unguarded. Since they were the same team that was assigned to him in England they felt quite at ease in the party, and on painting and picnic excursions they pitched in and helped like everyone else. Also present was a valet, who not only dressed Churchill and looked after his other needs in the bedroom, but squeezed the tube when his master wanted more paint, saw that a fresh cigar was never more than a few feet away, and did hundreds of other little things which added to his comfort. To help him with his *Memoirs*, as well as to keep him company, Churchill brought relays of historians, researchers and military advisers who were part-time members of his London staff. Sometimes his doctor, Lord Moran, would be invited for a week or ten days even when Mr Churchill was in the best of health. At other times he turned for companionship to someone like Sir Oswald Birley, the portrait painter, who died some years before Churchill did; and once he asked an obscure Swiss artist, who many years earlier had taught him some of the rudiments of painting, to spend three or four weeks with him in Morocco. The rest of the party was usually members of the family. Mrs Churchill stayed for the duration when possible, while the daughters came for a week or two at a time.

Though Churchill's holidays were even less formal, if that is possible, than his private life in England, the day's activities were highly organized. There was little time that anyone had to himself, and no one felt that it was really polite to go his own way. An exception was breakfast, which was not a group affair, but which everyone ordered in his room when he pleased. There was always the danger, however, that Churchill might have risen early, and be ready to start doing something before

certain members of the party had finished their *café complet*, so no one dared to order breakfast for much later than 8.30. Much depended on the weather: if it were fine, Churchill wanted to get an expedition under way early; when it was cloudy, he was content to stay indoors and wait for the sun to emerge. As a rule a secretary would telephone all members of the party around 9 a.m. and divulge the plans for the day. 'Lunch will be at 1.30. No guests. Mrs Churchill is going to the Zoo at 11, and would be glad if you could go with her. Oh, yes, the Mayor and his wife, a Mr and Mrs Pages, are coming to dinner. They have been asked for 8. You will all meet in the sitting-room at 7.40.' The ladies were also told whether they were to wear long or short dresses in the evening. (It was a standing rule that the men were to appear in dinner jackets, although Churchill only applied the rule to himself when some head of state or royal prince turned up. Normally he wore a zip suit.)

The plans, however, might change so often during the course of the day that the established form of greeting among the younger members of the party was always, 'Well, what's the drill?'

A feature of every holiday was the picnic, a daily event if the weather permitted, and a command performance for everyone in the party. Churchill's picnics were star turns, and he expected all his guests to attend.

Probably no man in the twentieth century organized an outing on such a lavish scale. The site was selected some days in advance, after Mrs Churchill or another person had explored the region with a careful eye on what would make good subjects for Mr Churchill's brush. Sometimes a site fifty miles from the hotel would be chosen.

Departure time was usually at 11 sharp. About two minutes earlier the whole party, with the exception of Churchill, had arranged themselves in their automobiles. The moment Churchill appeared, the cavalcade set forth, and quite a cavalcade it was. First there would be a police car with two or three local policemen. Then the Churchill car would follow, trailed by four or five automobiles bearing the other guests. After them came the food van, containing, as well as the food and drink, a couple of full-sized tables, an adequate number of chairs, Churchill's easel and painting equipment, and Churchill's valet. After that came the detectives, and, often, after that, another detachment of native police.

Churchill preferred fast driving to slow, but the pace invariably set by the local police, who thought their duty was to get Churchill to his destination as quickly as possible, must have frightened him more than once. Careless speed also annoyed him. Once when his driver, racing through the dusty desert in Morocco, struck a sheep, Churchill stopped the car, growled at the driver, sympathized with the shepherd, and gave him 500 francs.

When the picnic site was reached, everything stopped while Churchill looked around for the best place to set up his easel. Sometimes this took fifteen or twenty minutes. Then he went to work, a whisky and soda having been poured for him in the meantime. Twenty or thirty yards away from him the tables were set up and covered with white cloths, the chairs placed and the food laid out. For everyone there was an individually-packed lunch which the hotel had spent the early part of the morning preparing, and which consisted usually of an assortment of chicken breasts, cold roast beef and York ham, rolls and butter,

rich cakes, fruit and several kinds of cheese. Champagne flowed copiously throughout the meal, and there was port for the cheese and brandy for the coffee.

But in spite of the sumptuousness of the fare, the police guard, the formal table-setting and the little band of natives that invariably clustered a courteous hundred or so yards away, the picnics were as gay and easy as those of any ordinary large and good-humoured family. There were no guests and polite attendants: with the exception of Mr Churchill, who painted busily away with sublime disregard for the bustle going on behind him, everyone, from Mrs Churchill and assorted elderly peers and generals down, pitched in to help the detectives and Norman the valet, get things in readiness, and everyone hopped up and down from the table as often as he pleased to get what he wanted of food and drink. Everyone laughed, everyone was unbraced.

If the sun got hot, you put your napkin on your head, turban style, and the others would follow suit, joking inordinately at the strange effects produced. If you got even hotter, you could take off your shirt, for all anybody would care.

Gayest and most unbraced of the company was always Churchill, who on picnics became more roguish and ebullient than ever, and delighted in singing old songs, telling slightly *risqué* stories and pressing drink ('It's *white* port, you know. All the ladies must have some because it's only *white* port') on everyone round him.

At Marrakech he took special delight in a couple of picnic customs which he quickly elevated to the rank of formal ceremonies. One was the drinking of old Indian Army toasts, which he had learned from his friend and

assistant, General Sir Henry Pownall; and at the end of every picnic we would solemnly rise and drink the Toast for the Day. On Sundays it was 'To Absent Friends,' on Mondays, 'To Men,' and so on through 'To Women,' 'To Religion,' 'To Our Swords,' 'To Ourselves,' 'To Wives and Sweethearts,' to the end of the week.

The other was a verse from Thomas Gray's 'Ode on the Spring,' which he gravely recited at each picnic:

> 'Beside some water's rushy brink
> With me the Muse shall sit and think
> (At ease reclined in rustic state)
> How vain the ardour of the Crowd,
> How low, how little are the Proud,
> How indigent the great.'

One night at dinner my wife asked him to repeat the verse to her. 'Oh, no, I couldn't,' he replied firmly. 'I can only say it at picnics.'

After lunch Churchill was left to himself for two or three hours while the others would go off with Mrs Churchill to visit an ancient ruin, inspect a native village or call on a local chieftain. On their return they usually found that in some mysterious manner a large crowd had collected on the picnic ground. They would be standing stock-still in a huge semi-circle behind Churchill, talking only in respectful whispers, while he painted away, completely oblivious to everything except the scene in front of him.

Sometimes the visitors could not be ignored. There was the time, for example, in Provence, when the Mayor of the nearest village and half his town council came to the picnic grounds bearing a huge chain to which was attached the key to the village. Since Churchill was completely absorbed

in his painting and would not even so much as turn his head to look at the delegation that had come to honour him, Mrs Churchill, on her return, had to be at her diplomatic best. Sometimes she even persuaded her husband to favour the visitors with a word, a handshake and a smile when, as the light began to fail, he was ready anyway to pack up and go back to the hotel for a snooze before dinner.

Churchill's happiest and most successful holidays were probably those spent in Marrakech, the romantic town in the interior of Morocco, 150 miles from Casablanca. It satisfied just about all of Churchill's tastes for the best, although he nearly died there a couple of times from pneumonia, which he probably got from the sudden drop in temperature after sunset. Churchill liked Marrakech because it was far away from the hurly-burly of the political world in which he was caught up during the rest of the year. The deep blue sky, the white Atlas Mountains and the rich red earth appealed to the artist in him more than any other country he knew. And though in most respects Marrakech is a thousand years behind the times—an aspect which Churchill also liked—the town possesses a hotel, the Mamounia, which provided Churchill with every luxury and comfort his heart desired.

On most visits to Marrakech Churchill stayed pretty close to town and the surrounding forty or fifty miles of countryside at the foot of the mountains. He made paintings of the old walls and towers, of transactions in the bazaar, of views of the city from high points nearby, and sometimes he went no farther afield than the Mamounia gardens of orange trees, palms and bougainvillea. But on his last visit, with a chartered four-engined Skymaster standing by at the airport two minutes away, he yielded to

the desire that had probably gripped him from the moment he first saw Marrakech. What was it like on the other, the Sahara, side of the Atlas Mountains?

He had heard that just over the range there was an interesting village, named Tinerhir, where he could establish headquarters at a small hotel under the same management as the Mamounia, and that from there painting expeditions could easily be organized into a valley of fascinating villages and into magnificent gorges of red stone and marble.

Ordinarily Churchill did not like to make risky flights, and flying over the Atlas, 12,000 feet straight up from the Marrakech airport, was hardly a safe thing to do. There was also the question of finding a suitable landing strip on the other side. But Churchill was blind to danger when he really craved something.

On the first flight the pilot got Churchill over the mountains successfully, but when he took a look at the short, sandy strip at Tinerhir he refused to risk a landing with Churchill aboard, so he flew thirty or forty miles farther on to a better strip. Churchill completed the rest of the journey by car, while the aircraft went back and took another look at Tinerhir. After one or two attempts a landing was made. Churchill was enchanted with the region, stayed a few days, and returned to Marrakech to plan the next trip with more supplies and more people.

Churchill's last flight to Tinerhir, one that my wife and I made with him, might easily have ended in disaster. There were fourteen people in the plane, including Mrs Churchill, one of the daughters, Diana, a cousin, a secretary, a valet and the crew. Churchill always smoked on take-offs if he felt like it, but this time, as the plane

WITH LORD CHERWELL AT THE FONTAINE DE VAUCLUSE,
PROVENCE

raced down the runway, he decided to take no chances, and tried to ram his burning six-inch cigar into the receptacle on the arm of his chair. When he found that the cigar was too big for the ashtray, he lifted the metal container out of the arm, deposited the cigar in the hole, replaced the container, and settled down for a snooze.

Hardly had the plane left the ground and started the sharp climb over the Atlas when the smell of a burning cigar permeated the cabin and a cloud of smoke enveloped Churchill. He was the first to realize that something was wrong and called for the stewardess. Together they discovered the source of the fire, and in a few minutes enough water was poured down the hole to extinguish it. By this time Churchill had become frightened, and was determined to make doubly sure that the fire was really out. Grabbing his steel-pronged walking-stick he proceeded to ram it down the hole and bash the cigar at the bottom. Still not satisfied, he sent for one of the officers of the aircraft and demanded that the cigar be retrieved. When this was done he announced: 'Now we can go over the mountain.'

The next day Churchill proposed a flight farther south, to the edge of the Sahara. When the rest of the party expressed visible coolness (it would have meant sending the Skymaster all the way back to Marrakech to get extra fuel) Churchill moped: 'I have half a notion to go by myself. Why should I submit to mob rule of this kind!'

Once settled in Tinerhir, however, Churchill was blissfully happy and worked at his easel with feverish energy all day long. The hotel was tiny, hardly more than a hostel, so Churchill was able to ignore the one or two other guests and do exactly as he pleased. At every meal the dining-

F

room was converted into a studio, and lined with all the paintings he had started. And, except when the commandant of the Tinerhir garrison, or the governor of the region, was his guest, Churchill would eat his food in complete silence, brooding lovingly over creations, and pondering on the effects he still wanted to achieve.

He brought back at least a dozen pictures from his few days at Tinerhir, all to be completed during the dark days of an English winter.

# CHAPTER EIGHT

# CHURCHILL'S

# HOUSES

Duning the time I knew him, Churchill shifted about between four residences: his two official houses—10 Downing Street and Chequers—his town house at 28 Hyde Park Gate, and Chartwell. But he had only one real home, and that was Chartwell, his country estate about twenty-five miles from London, in the rolling Weald of Kent and not far from Biggin Hill, the famous flying field from which, during the war, planes took off to fight the Battle of Britain. Chartwell was the spot he really loved, the place where he was always happiest. Often after a late session in the House he would drive out at midnight, through the dreary, impoverished miles of south-east London, just to be there for a few hours before returning to town for lunch.

Except for its spacious grounds behind the house, Chartwell could hardly have been more unlike the ordinary idea of what a stately English country house should be. From the outside, the massive red-brick two-storey building of indeterminate architectural style was stately enough, though there was no long, avenued approach to its entrance, but only a curved gravel driveway separating it from the road. Once inside the huge weatherbeaten front door,

however, the house showed, as did everything belonging to him, its own marks of Churchillian eccentricity.

The ground floor was hardly a living floor at all, and no room fulfilled its original function. To the right of the entrance hall, what had once been a reception room had been turned into a bedroom and bathroom-dressing-room for Mrs Churchill. The big main drawing-room, with its tall windows and ample light, had become Churchill's studio and was filled almost to the chandeliers with stacks of pictures, easels and paint-daubed palettes. Another room had been made into an office for the secretaries. It, too, was usually a bit of a jumble, crowded as it was with books, manuscripts, dispatch boxes, teacups, two or three secretaries—and sometimes Churchill himself if he chose to spend a little time there.

The entrance hall contained a table or so, some chairs, half a dozen hats, walking-sticks, a visitors' book, which Churchill always tried to remember to get guests to sign, but usually forgot, lots of coats and various mackintoshs, slippers and boots for Churchill to slip in or out of as he entered or left the house. The rest of the floor was given over to the kitchens and 'the usual offices.'

It was on the first floor that the family really lived, ate and slept, and for this purpose it had been converted into an almost self-contained flat. Even here, however, there was no grandeur, but only solid, tasteful comfort. The little hall, which was really more of a corridor, looked almost cottagey with its gay flowered wallpaper, but the big living-room, once, no doubt, the master bedroom, was elegant enough with its soft, pastel colours, barrelled ceiling, large fireplace and deep windows looking out over the valley to the Kentish hills beyond. The dining-

room, also once a bedroom, was much smaller, and no more than eight could sit down to table with comfort.

Churchill's own bedroom looked south, so that from his windows he could view the gardens and the countryside. Next to it was his study, which contained a large black table for a desk and a roughly-hewn sideboard, on which he could spread his galleys and manuscripts. During most of the year a fire burned brightly in the study fireplace, and Churchill would often tend to it himself, blowing at it belligerently with his bellows and muttering, 'That's better like it,' as the flames rose higher.

The other bedrooms were all very small and there were not enough of them for guests. Not for the Churchills the time-honoured English week-end house-party. Chartwell was a place for peace and recuperation.

The stairs from the first to the ground floor were very curved and slippery, and more than one distinguished guest has gone down them on his backside in spite of Churchill's constant warnings to be careful. 'You must grasp the hand-cord *very* tightly,' he would often say, peering anxiously over the railing at the departing visitor. Or he would lead the way himself, 'and then, if you should slip, I shall stop your fall.' After his stroke in 1953 Churchill had a lift installed.

Though Churchill had two detectives in constant attendance on him at Chartwell, as everywhere else, they never seemed to be in evidence when a visitor drove into the driveway. In fact, nobody was, and nothing could have been more casual than one's entrance into this great man's abode. For unless he were a very important dignitary for whom a special welcome was essential, the visitor simply walked up to the door, opened it (it was never locked),

walked in and hoped that sooner or later he would come across someone he knew. Perhaps a secretary would appear, bearing a pile of papers, and stop to greet him. Or Randolph would come stomping down the stairs, peer vaguely into the gloom and say, 'Oh, hello. I think father's in his study.'

The day that the attempt was made to assassinate Truman, I was visiting Chartwell and could not help wondering a little at the nonchalance which prevailed. The hall was empty, so I walked to the office, hoping to find someone there. But there was not a soul, though plenty of open black cases lay about, with important-looking documents inside. Finally Mrs Churchill's secretary entered, asked where everyone was and said, 'I'd better go and find Mr Churchill myself,' since she was quite sure he had awakened from his nap. I then went upstairs and wandered through the halls to his study, still without meeting a detective or anyone else on the way.

Only once, in fact, did I ever come across a detective inside the house. I was having more difficulty than usual trying to find someone astir, and had travelled down several corridors in my vain search. Finally I took a wrong turning that led me down to the basement, and there he was—seated on his bed carefully cleaning his revolver.

The grounds were Chartwell's greatest glory and Churchill's special pride. 'This is one of the loveliest sights of England,' he would say as he sat on his lawn behind the house and pointed to the valleys and hills around him, the black swans preening themselves in the pond below, and the cattle grazing peacefully on the sloping meadows. It was indeed a beautiful spot and nothing had been left undone to make it still more

beautiful. There were rose gardens, kitchen gardens and greenhouses, rockeries and flag-stoned terraces, fish-ponds, duck-ponds, swimming-pools and waterfalls, a little pavilion decorated with bas reliefs of Marlborough and the Battle of Blenheim (done by his artist-nephew, John Churchill), masses of rhododendron everywhere and all manner of trees and flowering shrubs.

Much of the work on the place had been done by Churchill himself. A plaque in the mellow brick walls of the big kitchen garden proclaimed that Winston Churchill had built it. Many of the estate's cottages were also the result of his own labour. But the creation in which he took the most pride was a complicated water system by which water was piped up the hill from the pond in the valley and used for the heated swimming-pool, the fish-ponds and the little cascades which splashed down through the artificial rockeries. Churchill designed and supervised the whole installation and did a good deal of the work besides.

Even when he could no longer actively participate in his engineering schemes, nothing was ever done without his expert sidewalk supervision. He always had some project or other on hand for the improvement of his estate, and one would often hear half-laughing, half-exasperated complaints from the rest of the family about the activities of 'Father's bulldozer.'

If Chartwell was Mr Churchill's special haven, the town house at 28 Hyde Park Gate was more Mrs Churchill's domain. The rooms were bigger, grander and more richly decorated, the servants in greater evidence, and the whole house seemed designed to provide a fitting background for an eminent public figure. But it was far from being

ostentatious. It was situated in a not very fashionable section of London, in a secluded dead-end street, and, from the outside, looked as if it might have belonged to any moderately successful stockbroker or lawyer.

Churchill bought No. 28 shortly after he lost the 1945 election. Later he bought No. 27 as well, and turned the two houses into one. In No. 27 were located the secretaries' offices, and rooms for his assistants when they came from time to time to help him on his books. When Churchill returned to office in 1951, he let No. 28 to the Cuban Ambassador, but kept No. 27 for his own use. On his retirement he again moved into No. 28.

There was always a policeman somewhere or other in Hyde Park Gate, but he gave the impression of being just about as casual as Chartwell's detective. He seldom got nearer than a hundred feet to the house, and, though he would look vaguely at all the cars entering the little cul-de-sac, it was a continual mystery to me how he could have sensed or stopped any attempt at foul play.

It was a great wrench for Churchill to abandon, in 1951, his well-loved private houses for the official grandeur of 10 Downing Street and Chequers. And, in fact, he resisted the change as long as he could. For a whole year after the elections he lived in Downing Street as Mr Attlee had done, in a small, self-contained flat, such as he was used to at Chartwell, at the top of the house. It was not until late in 1952 that the family moved down into their proper prime ministerial grandeur and took over the stately reception rooms on the lower floors for their living quarters.

It was even more difficult for him to get used to Chequers again. At first he disliked it so much that he insisted on spending his week-ends at Chartwell, except when an

official house-party or a Cabinet conference made his attendance there obligatory. In the first three or four months of his prime ministership he went only twice to Chequers. But as the year progressed and his duties as official entertainer gathered momentum (Mrs Churchill also found it an increasingly arduous task to keep two country mansions running smoothly), Chartwell was reluctantly given up and Chequers, with its gloomy vastness, cold halls and heavy Victorian furniture, became his only week-end home.

But though Chartwell was shut up and never used by the other members of the family, Churchill himself could not leave it entirely. One room was kept open for his use, and often he would slip down there on a Friday night to take a quick look at the old familiar place before starting off for the pomp of his official residence.

# CHAPTER NINE

## CHURCHILL'S

## HOBBIES

CHURCHILL was richly endowed with that rare gift, though not uncommon among great men, of being able to put aside work and worries, and find relaxation in hobbies. The older he got the more he had, because it was not his way to drop an old love for a new one. And true to his character he did not take on a hobby in any half-hearted fashion; it was serious business, something to be enjoyed in full measure.

His love for painting never waned, although during the last few years of his life he hardly used a single English scene for a subject. His system was to start so many paintings on holidays abroad that he would have plenty to keep him busy in England until the next time he went abroad. He never, to my knowledge, attempted a portrait, but from time to time he would paint a still life, like a water lily next to a black figurine that someone had sent him from a remote corner of the world.

He treasured his collection as a boy loves a bag of marbles, not for their intrinsic value but because they were his own. Of the hundreds of paintings that he completed in his lifetime not more than half a dozen or so ever left his possession for good. Even his son and daughters were not

given pictures for keeps. Their constant worry when he came to see them was that he would spy one of his pictures, and say: 'That's very good. I'd like to have that back if you don't mind.'

He derived infinite pleasure from looking at his collection over and over again, and he loved showing it to friends, particularly if they left him in no doubt as to their high regard for his skill. He had an enchanting way of making someone visiting Chartwell for the first time feel signally honoured. He would invite the guest into his studio and ask him to sit in a chair very close to his own, facing a wall covered with paintings. Then for a few minutes he would fall into a meditative mood, thoughtfully regarding the quality of the blue in his Moroccan sky or peacefully closing his eyes for half a minute.

The silence was always broken in one of two ways. By far the more preferable to Churchill was an exclamation from his visitor concerning the beautiful shadow effects he had achieved in that river scene. 'Do tell me where you painted this lovely picture?' a satisfactory visitor would ask. That was enough to get Churchill started on a half-hour's lively discourse and discussion about his paintings, during the course of which he would carefully ask his visitor's opinion on many points. If, by ill luck, his visitor was not the responsive type, Churchill would have to break the silence himself. 'I'm not quite satisfied with the wall in that one over there. Difficult to get it just right. So much detail, and then the sun changes everything so fast.' He would then hopefully look for some kind of response.

Churchill was certainly proud of his ability to paint. He enjoyed being in the company of artistic people like Sir John

Rothenstein of the Tate Gallery, and took very seriously his membership of the Royal Academy; but it is debatable whether he really considered himself much better than an amateur.

I remember a remark he made at dinner once in Aix-en-Provence after a long, happy afternoon in the Cezanne country painting Mont St. Victoire. Deep in thought for several minutes, he suddenly broke into the conversation around him, and said rather gravely:

'I have had a wonderful life, full of many achievements. Every ambition I've ever had has been fulfilled—save one.'

'Oh, dear me, what is that?' said Mrs Churchill.

'I am not a *great* painter,' he said, looking slowly around the table. For a few seconds the embarrassment was so complete that no one could bring himself to say anything, and then the party talked of other things.

Churchill became interested in race-horses shortly after the end of the Second World War, partly through the influence of his son-in-law, Christopher Soames. This hobby in its own way became almost as engrossing as painting, and at the height of the season Churchill often went to some lengths to organize his appointments so they would not conflict with his visits to the track. Once he flew back from Denmark in the morning, to Liverpool for lunch, back to London, then fifty miles by air to Newmarket to see one of his horses run in the 4.20.

When Colonist II was at the top of his form, confounding the betting experts with sensational victories at some of the biggest races in England, Churchill was often in daily communication with his trainer, Nightingall. A long telephone call to Lord Woolton about the strategy to be

employed in an important by-election was sometimes
followed by an equally long conversation with Nightingall
on how Colonist looked in the morning workout.

Race-horses were a particularly satisfying hobby because
next to spending money he liked nothing so much as
making it. His horses made him a pile. In one year alone
his winnings from purses and bets exceeded £10,000. 'And
don't forget,' Churchill would exclaim, 'a thousand pounds
made out of horses is equivalent to twenty thousand in
normal business enterprise at to-day's rate of taxation. I
don't have to pay taxes on my thousand because it's called
a capital gain or some such thing.'

He loved to bet on his own horses, and usually inveigled
all his friends into doing the same. I remember Lord
Camrose telephoning once to congratulate him when
Colonist II had made a particularly spectacular win. 'Oh,'
replied Churchill from the other end, 'you're to be congratulated, too. I put £50 on him for you, and you've just
made £200.' If Colonist had lost, Camrose would have
received a bill—but Churchill never ventured more than
he thought his friends could afford to lose. To him I was
worth only ten pounds each way.

Later in his life Churchill's wealth enabled him to
make a hobby of farming. His first move was to buy
up half a dozen small farms bordering on Chartwell, which
up till then was comparatively small. Next he appointed
Christopher Soames, who had married his youngest and
favourite daughter, Mary, as manager. Soon a market
garden was in full swing, and nice ripe Churchill tomatoes
began to appear at Covent Garden. After Churchill bought
a tractor he found pleasure in having a king of tractors,
Harry Ferguson, and one of his experts, out for lunch and

the afternoon to discuss the famous Ferguson method of farming. He bought a hundred or so head of dairy cattle and a prize bull, sold most of his belted Galloways when he learned that they were being bred at a loss.

The time he placed a blind advertisement in an English paper to sell his bull he was soon confronted with a problem in diplomacy.

'I've got to attend a meeting over at Christopher's office,' he said to me one day in the middle of a walk. 'We have to decide something about the bull. Come along.'

'What are we going to do?' said Soames, when Churchill and a farm assistant had seated themselves around the bare wooden table. 'We *can't* sell to the *Russians*.'

'Very difficult,' Churchill replied after a few minutes' thought. 'Do you think the Russians know the bull belongs to me?'

'Probably not,' said Soames. 'Their intelligence can't be *that* good. After all, the advertisement only gave a box number.'

'We cannot discriminate against the Russians over a bull,' Churchill finally decided. 'That would not be fair.' Then, with a twinkle in his eye, he added: 'But they'll have to pay a good price to get it. I'm not going to have that poor fellow sent to Russia for nothing.'

The Russian inquiry was politely answered, with a price tag that forced them out of the bidding.

Churchill never became an expert on agriculture, but, as in all things that interested him, he applied good common sense and absorbed enough knowledge to be able to make reasonably sound judgments. He knew the value of crop rotation, and he could discuss methods employed

for increasing the alfalfa yield. As soon as he acquired a new farm he had a long talk with the family that had been farming it, invited them to stay on and work for him, and took steps to modernize and improve the farmhouse and other buildings. He also became a member of the Kent County Agricultural Society, and attended their annual show when possible.

Bricklaying was a hobby that Churchill abandoned after he had completed all the walls and cottages that he wanted. He also found the work a little exhausting in later life. Nevertheless, about once a year he did mix a little mortar and clap a few bricks together just to prove to himself that he had not lost the art. He likewise found the strain too great, as the years passed, to build new reservoirs or repair his swimming-pool. Towards the end he left all the actual labour to others while he directed operations from the sidelines.

The wonders of the miniature camera began to fascinate Churchill after the war when it occurred to him that if he could record a scene in black or white, better still in colour, he would have a wonderful guide always at hand for the scene he was painting. The Professor, Lord Cherwell, himself a great camera enthusiast, was called in. He recommended the purchase of a Leica, and offered to show Churchill how to use it.

The Leica was bought, but the course of instruction did not get very far because the pupil became impatient with all the little gadgets and screws. Churchill then arranged for a couple of his secretaries to be taught the rudiments of photography. Meanwhile the Professor went to work designing and installing in the studio at Chartwell an elaborate device which enabled Churchill to have an

enlargement of his film on a screen right beside his easel. When he showed me the installation he said, a little apologetically: 'It helps me to refresh my memory. I, of course, give everything my own interpretation. But I'd rather you didn't talk too much about this equipment.'

*Frank Scherschel – Life*

WITH MRS CHURCHILL IN PROVENCE

# CHAPTER TEN

# CHURCHILL'S

# ANIMALS

'THE world would be better off if it were inhabited only by animals,' Churchill said the morning one of his beloved black swans was found killed by a fox. He was in the depths of despair. It made no difference that his remark was fantastically absurd. He preferred to ignore the fact that the fox is also an animal. His way of expressing his love for the swan was to damn the whole human race.

The black swans, natives of New Zealand and presented to Churchill by that nation, lived in a small lake in the valley about 300 yards behind the big house at Chartwell. They could be seen swimming about from the windows on either side of the fireplace in the main drawing-room. I arrived for lunch a few minutes after the news of the tragedy was brought to Churchill. All the colour had left his face, his jaw was set, and his eyes were flooded with tears. 'Poor, poor thing,' he said over and over again as he paced the room, first looking out of one window towards the lake and then out of the other. It was as if he half-expected the fox to return again or the dead swan to come back to life.

After a while, Christopher Soames came to report

details of the attack. A little breathlessly he explained that the fox had evidently found its way to the lake through the woods in the early morning. It was resisted by the mother swan who was bent on protecting her young, hatched a few weeks before, at all costs. Soames declared, much to his father-in-law's satisfaction ('I knew she would'), that the mother swan had given the fox a fight he would long remember, and that, but for her courageous defence, the whole family might have been killed.

Churchill felt a little better after receiving this news, and began to discuss steps necessary to avoid a repetition of the tragedy. First, the swans would have to be removed that very day to the Regent's Park Zoo, where they would be safe, and where they could be looked after now that they no longer had a mother. Second, a system of defence in depth was to be constructed which would make it next to impossible for a fox or any other attacker to penetrate as far as the lake. (Within a few days a most intricate arrangement of wire nets and fences was put down, and the whole region was floodlighted at night. The swans were taken off to the Zoo for a month, where they received periodic visits from their owner.)

His instructions given, Churchill felt composed enough to go in to lunch. For a time the champagne revived his spirits, but he hardly touched his food. He attempted to talk, first about politics, then about his books, but he always lapsed into gloomy silence, and if not that, talk always led to the black swan and the fox. He was almost overcome with grief.

He tried again to be cheerful, saying, 'I will be all right to-morrow. This day will be bad for me, but I can't go on mourning day after day.' But it was no use. After barely

sampling the brandy he led the way to the drawing-room for another look out of the window towards the lake. Churchill was obviously exhausted and wanted to be alone, so I said I had to get back to town. 'You must forgive me,' he said, looking more kindly than I had ever seen him look before. 'I'm afraid I wasn't much good to-day. You must come down again in a few days.'

Later that afternoon I had an appointment with Herbert Morrison, the then Lord President of the Council, at No. 11 Downing Street, and related the experience at Chartwell. Although Morrison at that time was a bitter political enemy of Churchill's and, next to Aneurin Bevan, tried more than anyone to discomfit him in the House of Commons, he forgot all animosities for the next few minutes, took up pen and paper and wrote Churchill a note of condolence.

More than a year later Churchill, talking at dinner of Herbert Morrison, recalled the letter he had received from him the morning after the black swan tragedy. 'That was a kind thing to do,' he said. 'Old Herbert is really a good fellow. I wonder how he heard about my misfortune so quickly after it happened.'

But all was not peace in the lake even after it was fortified. When the baby black swans grew up, jealousies arose and they began fighting among themselves. It then became necessary to divide the lake into sections (through the use of more wire fencing), one for each of three factions. Thereafter, every afternoon he was at Chartwell, Churchill marched from one warring camp to the other to see how they were getting on and to feed them bits from the huge pieces of bread he and his detectives took down to them.

About the time of the black swan incident Churchill

suffered further grief over the death of perhaps his closest animal friend. Rufus was a chocolate-coloured miniature French poodle, lively and smart as anything, and he adored Mr Churchill. 'See, he kisses me,' Churchill would say as Rufus hopped on to his bed, over the bed-table and settled on his chest. 'I didn't come to know the dog world until late in life. No one should not know the companionship of a dog. There is nothing like it. But dogs never really liked me very much. Rufie, you're just learning to. Darling Rufie.'

Then one Saturday afternoon Churchill went to Brighton to make a wind-up speech at a Conservative Party conference, and took Rufie along. While he was speaking Rufie was taken for a walk. Allowed off his leash, he darted across the street into the path of a bus, and was killed. Churchill heard the news after he finished speaking. It was a painful blow and, tears filling his eyes, he asked that the body be taken to Chartwell for burial. There is now a stone in the garden marking Rufie's grave.

The next time I saw Churchill he was getting acquainted with Rufie II whom I had found at the same kennels which produced Rufie I, and who was almost an exact duplicate. 'I think he's very sweet,' said Churchill, happy once more. 'But I'd like to try living together for a while before coming to a permanent arrangement. Matrimony is a serious state to enter upon. We both must see how we get along with one another.'

So for the next few weeks Rufie II and Churchill were on trial, and although Rufie suffered the handicap of not knowing it, Churchill thoughtfully made due allowances, and the association prospered. Mrs Churchill hoped that nothing would come of the affair, not because she disliked

dogs but because she did not think her husband had the time and patience a dog required. 'When you're in the House of Commons,' she said, 'you can't take him with you; when you're writing you don't want to be disturbed. You can't take him abroad; and even when you're in England you can't have him both in town and in the country.'

The decision was almost not left to Churchill at all. The trial arrangement had not been going for more than a few weeks when Rufie came down with a serious attack of distemper, which left him with a bad quiver in his right leg. 'I'm afraid the marriage can't take place,' said Churchill mournfully. 'We've had the doctor over, and he says there is no hope that the leg will get right again.'

Rufie was then taken back to the kennels, but some days later, just as I was making arrangements to take Rufie into my own home, word came that Churchill had asked for him to be brought over again. His attachment had become too strong, even if Rufie was a cripple. 'I'm going to see how it works,' Churchill said the next time I saw him. 'I'm not sure whether I'll keep him or not, but we'll see.'

Rufie stayed, until his death at the age of 15. After about two years his leg was almost normal. He could run as fast as the next poodle, and he liked nothing so much as to chase rubber balls thrown as far as his master's arm could heave them. He never, however, became completely house-trained, and even at dignified Chequers a guest was quite likely to come upon one of Rufie's messes while passing through the stately halls.

Yet the friendship grew, and though at first Rufie barked frequently and perhaps because of Churchill's many absences often preferred to stay at the valet's cottage down

the road (where he also had a lady friend), he soon became accustomed to Churchill's extraordinary life. He was probably happiest at mealtime, when he was allowed to sit on a chair very near the table at Mr Churchill's side. Every few minutes Churchill would turn and look at him affectionately. 'Poor darling, come and talk to me,' he would say tenderly three or four times during lunch or dinner.

Much later in life he tried to become attached to the Chartwell cat, a species of animal he had previously ignored. Then another chair appeared in the dining-room, and Mr Churchill would hold court with Rufie on his right and the big brindled tom, Micky, on his left. For some time he took great pride in this new satellite and one day became very angry with William Deakin, his long-time assistant, because Deakin began to tease the cat and made it jump from its chair beside him.

But the cat relationship never really flourished: Micky refused to give Mr Churchill the whole-hearted devotion he wanted, and after a while retreated into his old kitchen haunts. Some months later Churchill could not even remember his name. 'Oh, that awful old Turkey cat,' he replied when once I asked after him. 'I never could get that cat to like me, you know, though I tried so hard. I haven't seen him for weeks now.'

Churchill was almost as fond of his golden carp as he was of Rufie, the cat, and the black swans. He kept hundreds of them in a pool which he had built himself between the two wars near his house at Chartwell, and every day after lunch he went down to look at them and feed them. 'Hike, Hike—Hike, Hike,' he would always shout the moment he had seated himself on the little green chair in

the shade at the edge of the pool. 'See, they can hear me. Look how they're all coming towards me. Now we'll give them something to eat.' Then he would heave a few dozen maggots into the pond, and watch the fish dart for them. 'Aristocratic maggots, these are,' he sometimes said. 'Look how well the fish are doing on them.' After more 'hike, hikes' and a few dozen maggots he would move on.

Some years after the war Churchill also began keeping tropical fish, an interest which began when an admiring English youngster sent a few to Chartwell with a letter saying that he thought Churchill might be amused to watch them play and grow. At first a tank was rigged up in the basement, and from time to time Churchill remembered to return from a walk via the basement so that he could see how they were getting along. People around the house also added to the collection.

But before long the inevitable happened. Another new world opened itself to Churchill. New tanks were ordered, not one, but four, all richly decorated with stones and plants. And they were installed amid the sanctity of his study which up till then was a rather sombre room containing mostly books and trophies. The tanks were soon stocked with every rare variety that Churchill could get hold of. After that he never entered the room without first seating himself in front of the fish for twenty minutes or half an hour, exclaiming about their beauty, their antics, their love life, and calling them by name. And he could never resist the temptation of feeding them, far more than was good for them, from the small bottles that he kept near the tanks.

Even the ordinary farm animals got a goodly share of his interest and affection. On his walks across the rolling

fields of Chartwell, Churchill always paused to admire the beauty of the Belted Galloways, with their broad snow-white belts around dark-brown bodies. 'A sturdy animal, too,' Churchill would say. 'They have their young right there in the fields, even in the middle of winter.' When he would reach the herd of milk cows, mainly Jerseys, he would proudly demonstrate his cow-calling prowess. At the sound of their names the cows invariably came lumbering up to receive a pat from their owner.

He even had time for the lowly pig. He never passed the pens without saying a few words to the occupants and picking up the rake to give them a good back scratching.

# CHAPTER ELEVEN

# CHURCHILL'S

# FAMILY AND FRIENDS

CHURCHILL had a host of friends, some of whom he undoubtedly felt a deep affection for, but it was part of his character not to talk very much about other people, no matter how well he knew or loved them. He would talk endlessly about himself and what he was doing, but he displayed a slight, yet unmistakable, degree of weariness when the names of other personalities were mentioned. Nearly everyone of note, of course, claimed acquaintanceship, if not friendship, with him, and there were thousands at the time of his death who always referred to him as 'Winston' though they had never seen him in the flesh, and almost as many who had developed a Churchillian lisp just as good as his own. Every now and again when I went to see Mr Churchill I would mention the name of someone who I was certain had been to Chartwell for a visit, and almost without fail there was practically no response at all. I found this to be true even regarding members of his family. After trips to New York when, for example, I might have seen his daughter Sarah, he appeared to show no real interest on hearing the latest news about her. Yet, there could be no doubt about his love for his family, and it happened that Sarah was one of

his favourite daughters. I was once closely involved with a demonstration of Churchill's love for her. At the end of a holiday in Marrakech, Sarah and one or two others departed with me in a plane bound for Lisbon via Casablanca. We had scarcely taken off when heavy storms blew in from the Atlantic, making it impossible for us to reach Lisbon that day or to keep any kind of schedule. When Churchill, who was spending another night in Marrakech, learned of this, he promptly ordered communications to be opened with every British consulate and embassy south of Paris. About twenty-four hours later he was on the telephone to Sarah in a little restaurant in Lisbon, expressing joyous relief that she (and we) were safe. Later we learned that from the moment news had reached Marrakech that our plane was 'lost' Churchill could think of nothing else.

It was probably not in Churchill's make-up to lead a very social life. Shortly after we met I remember him saying, as I believe Marlborough said earlier, 'Surround yourself with as few people as possible.' Another time Sarah told me: 'You know, father doesn't really like to meet new people.' On one of the few occasions when I managed to get him to talk about President Roosevelt, he said: 'I could never run for President of the United States. All that handshaking of people I didn't give a damn about would kill me. Ten minutes here. Ten minutes there. . . . Not for me.'

The Churchills seldom had people staying with them overnight or for week-ends, and when anyone did it was usually a colleague like Anthony Eden or someone who was helping Churchill with his writings. Neither did the Churchills much enjoy visiting others. Although the owners of half the castles or country houses in England would have

turned their establishments inside out for the Churchills, the old gentleman was happier at home where he could do as he pleased. He did, however, spend a week-end every year or two at Windsor Castle with the Royal Family, and about once a year his cousins the Duke and Duchess of Marlborough persuaded him to spend a night or two at Blenheim Palace to see the room in which he was born. Some years before he died he also visited his great friend Lord Salisbury at Hatfield House in Hertfordshire, the famous old seat of the Cecil family. In the latter years of his life visits to public restaurants and clubs were almost unknown. Yet, within twenty-four hours after his stroke in 1953, he telephoned one of his closest friends to say that he was planning to attend the next dinner, about a fortnight later, of the Other Club, which was a small, exclusive organization to which he and a few intimate friends belonged.

Since he talked so little about the people he knew during his life, it is difficult to judge with any precision what his opinion was of even those he knew best. I am sure, however, that there can be no doubt of his extraordinary regard for at least two people in the last decades of his life. Both were soldiers, Lawrence of Arabia and George Catlett Marshall. But his observations to me even about them took only a few minutes. Of Lawrence he said: 'He was a genius. There is nothing that he couldn't have done had he lived— and had me behind him.' Of General Marshall he said: 'There you have the greatest soldier of them all.' No other military figures, as far as I could tell, were in the same class for him, although I have heard him speak highly of Montgomery, Wavell, Pound, Eisenhower, Portal, Alexander, Brooke and Ismay; the latter, always known

as Pug, having been perhaps his closest friend among all the soldiers he knew.

Churchill never seemed to wish to be drawn out in any conversation in which Roosevelt was mentioned, and I have never been able to tell whether this was because he grieved so much over the loss of a friend or whether the two had drifted apart towards the end of the President's life. I cannot remember Churchill ever saying more than one sentence in private which could have been a clue to his real opinion of the man: 'I always had the greatest respect and fondness for him,' was all he ever said to me. It is well known that he liked Roosevelt's aides, Harriman and Hopkins, although I have never heard him speak about either. In all the time that I knew him he never said what he thought of other leading politicians of his day, de Gasperi, Stalin, Molotov, Bidault, Adenauer. Among his fellow Englishmen there is no doubt, although I cannot recall the words he used, that he had a healthy respect and liking for Herbert Morrison and Ernest Bevin; and while he disagreed with their politics, and in some cases with their extremism, he admired the skill of Aneurin Bevan, Woodrow Wyatt and Michael Foot. Among his Party colleagues, although Eden was his closest friend, he at first had some reservations as to Eden's ability to lead the Conservative Party and to fill the office of Prime Minister. It was probably more this lack of complete confidence in his No. 2 man than any personal desire to stay in power that kept Churchill from resigning in the early 1950s. But as the years passed—especially following Eden's perform-ance at the Geneva Conference in 1954—Churchill lost his misgivings and gave Eden his full blessing and support. Of Maxwell Fyfe, now Lord Kilmuir, Churchill once said to

me: 'I have plans for him.' I took this to mean that he intended to promote him to higher office and in 1954, in fact, he was made Lord Chancellor. There were not many others whom I ever heard him discuss, though I knew of course that Lord Woolton and Walter Monckton were quite good friends. I believe that he had a high opinion of R. A. Butler's abilities, but my impression was that they were not personal friends.

Churchill's best friend in the latter part of his life was not a politician, although he was brought into the Government for several years. He was the late Lord Cherwell, the famous Oxford Professor, better known as Lindemann, and always called Prof by Churchill and everyone else who knew him. In a way it is surprising that he should have preferred the Prof's company to that of all others, because Churchill, no great student himself during his school days, frequently expressed impatience with the academic mind. The Prof himself often had to submit to lengthy leg-pulling and sometimes to rather sarcastic comments from the old man. But Churchill liked Cherwell's dry wit and keen mind, so whenever he relaxed in the country or abroad the Prof, in his bowler hat and black suit, was usually close at hand, and despite all the temptations he managed on these outings to adhere to a rigid diet which permitted no meat and practically no alcohol. Nevertheless, he always stayed up working or talking with Churchill far into the night. His death in 1957 brought deep grief to Churchill.

Another trusted friend was the late Lord Camrose, wealthy and distinguished owner of the *Daily Telegraph* and a string of magazines. Time and again in his long life Churchill turned to 'Bill,' as he always called him, for

advice, and there was probably no man with whom he shared so many of his thoughts and secrets. Both were intimate friends of the great 'F. E.' Smith, later Earl Birkenhead, whose son and daughter married two of Lord Camrose's children.

Among Churchill's other close friends were Lords Bracken and Beaverbrook, both of whom served him in the wartime Governments, both of whom were heavily engaged in the publishing business, and both of whom were unique in that they had the courage to speak up when they disagreed with Churchill. Lords Beaverbrook and Bracken also were less silent generally in Churchill's presence than most friends, but this quality did not necessarily help to endear them to him. If anything, Churchill liked his friends to be good listeners rather than good talkers, with of course moderate intelligence and a sense of humour (at least when Churchill told a joke). I remember one man, a painter from Switzerland, who spent about ten days with Churchill on a holiday without saying more than half a dozen words every day. Through meal after meal he sat in happy silence, aroused only when Churchill asked him a question from time to time.

Although he was happiest in a group of men, Churchill still found the time late in life to have good long visits with one or two of his best women friends. Lady Violet Bonham-Carter (now Lady Asquith), for example, spent a week-end at Chartwell with the Churchills, talking over old times and exchanging views on the events of the day. 'She has one of the finest brains in England and is the best woman speaker I know,' Churchill said to me at lunch when Lady Violet had left the table after getting the best of a long argument over the Black and Tans.

When King George VI died, Churchill was heavy with grief, as much because he had lost a good friend as because England had lost her King. On a number of occasions I heard him praise the King for the intense study he made of all the detail of government, and during the war for his great knowledge of every battlefront. 'A fine man,' Churchill often said. 'He worked very hard.' Churchill really looked forward to his weekly visits with the King throughout his terms of office, sought his advice, and sometimes acted on it.

On Elizabeth's succession, Churchill was a little inclined at first to treat her as a child Queen, with respect for her position but not for her mind. But as he saw more of her and observed her at work, especially in the preparations for the Coronation, his opinion changed. He discovered that the young Queen not only had a good brain but could be just as stubborn as the Prime Minister. And as the months passed Churchill came to love the Queen, and one of the ways he showed his affection was by having a huge photograph of her placed on a table at the foot of his bed in 10 Downing Street. It was the famous picture of her smiling out of her carriage window *en route* to Parliament. 'She is a fine and lovely woman,' he said to me one of the last times I saw him at Downing Street. 'She will be a great Queen. England can be proud of her.' There were tears in his eyes.

\*          \*          \*

A distinguished American lunched with the Churchills one day and came back with a discovery. 'Why have I heard so little about Mrs Churchill?' he said to me. 'I had no idea she was a woman of such beauty and charm, and I

am surprised that she hasn't become a famous person in her own right. We know so much, for instance, about Bess Truman and Mrs Roosevelt—what they look like, and what they do and say—and yet here is someone who is as much of a personality, if not more, and the public doesn't seem aware of her at all.'

But though Mrs Churchill all her life has remained in the background, as traditionally befits the wife of an English public man, in her own household her influence was all-pervasive. She was the perfect wife for Churchill, and it was probably as much due to her as anyone that he was able to accomplish so much in his later years.

Even when I knew her, she was a woman of remarkable beauty. Though in her sixties, she had the face and figure of someone twenty years younger, a flawless, unlined complexion and silken, immaculately-groomed white hair. She dressed with great elegance, usually in pastel colours, and even after a long and tiring journey was as trim as if she had just come from the hands of her lady's maid.

But her elegance and beauty were never frightening. She was invariably gracious, kind and simple in her manner and had a gift for putting people completely at their ease. Though highly intelligent she was not an intellectual, and while she naturally was interested in politics because of her husband's position, she did not engage in serious political discussions. Her conversation was easy and sprightly, but was concerned for the most part with small talk on household problems and the less momentous occurrences of the week. She had that gift, so vital in a politician's wife, of seeming intensely interested in all the affairs of the individual she happened to be talking to at the moment.

*Frank Scherschel — Life*

IN THE DINING-ROOM AT CHARTWELL, WITH RUFUS
AND A NAVAL ADVISER

She was not over-strong, and her job was a prodigious one. She had to keep several houses running smoothly for a husband who liked perfection in most things, but perhaps especially in his domestic arrangements. She had to entertain large numbers of people constantly and be a sympathetic hostess to as varied an assortment of humans as ever crossed a woman's threshold. And she had to keep calm and comfortable and happy a genius who was certainly not the easiest man in the world to cope with.

All these things she did admirably, and at a time when housekeeping, even for Prime Minister's wives, was not an easy matter. Often one would find her worrying about her servant problems just like any other ordinary British house-wife, and wondering whether the new cook would suit or whether the maids imported from Switzerland would turn out all right, or whether Winston's valet was not causing more trouble below stairs than he was giving satisfaction above. Once Mrs Churchill confessed to my wife that what she would really like, and what she hoped some day she might possess, was a small flat with three or four rooms and one maid. 'I would have to have a maid,' she said almost apologetically, 'I am getting too old now to do everything myself.'

In all her concerns Mr Churchill's comfort invariably predominated. There was never the slightest doubt for whom the household was run, why certain dishes were prepared, whose decision was always necessary for the slightest change in the day's routine. Churchill was the presiding genius in his house, just as he was in his country.

Mrs Churchill paid the greatest attention to his every wish, and particularly weighty was the question of his meals. My wife was with her once when she was discussing

H

Christmas dinner with the cook in her sitting-room at Chartwell. All went well until she had to decide whether Churchill would like his *pâté de foie gras* at the beginning or at the end of the meal. A decision of such moment could only be made by the master of the house, but as he was busy with his *Memoirs* at that time, it might be even more impolitic to disturb him. Mrs Churchill struggled with her dilemma for a few minutes, then decided that the *pâté* problem was quite important enough to justify her interrupting his work, and off she went to ask him. Even in such small things was his comfort paramount with his wife.

It was Mrs Churchill who organized the guests on holiday trips, keeping them continually occupied so that Churchill would have all the time he wanted for his painting or his literary and political work. She it was who received many of the local dignitaries and created goodwill for her husband by visiting minor sheiks or village mayors and mayoresses. During holidays at Marrakech she went bravely through rounds of picnics, long lunches and dinners with local potentates, though she was often suffering from attacks of lumbago.

It was touching to see the sympathy and deep affection between Churchill and his wife. Often brusque to others, he was invariably gentle and docile with her, and she on her side was always ready with a warm word or tender little joke to wheedle him into an expansive and jovial mood. She played to perfection her role of straight man to the star performer, and at any gathering was alert in prompting him to recite a song, tell a story or expound on some favourite topic. She was also at all times his most appreciative audience. Probably no woman could have

been a greater asset to her husband than she was to Churchill.

Randolph Churchill, the only son of the Churchills, was usually on pretty good terms with his father, whom he called 'father' in the presence of the great man and 'Winston' on most other occasions. It was only when Randolph became irrepressibly voluble at the luncheon or dinner table that relations became strained, and then Churchill would sometimes say: 'Randolph, I wish you would stop talking so much.'

Although Randolph will not equal his father's mark in history, he did inherit a great many Churchillian qualities. No one could fail to identify him as a Churchill in a crowd. He has his father's broad, sturdy build, the bull-dog expression, the large head, thick neck and girth, the blue eyes. His voice and manner of speaking remind one of his father, and his imitations, including the famous lisp, are probably more exact than most. Randolph is also endowed with a full quota of Churchillian courage. He fought on various fronts in World War II, and undertook a mission to Tito which called for parachuting a couple of times into the mountainous wilds of Jugoslavia. In Korea, where he went as a war correspondent, he was known as a fearless reporter, and on one of his trips to the front he was struck by a piece of shrapnel. This did not prevent him, however, from dictating his story from a hospital bed.

Churchill's three daughters, Sarah Beauchamp, Mary Soames and Diana Sandys, were alike mainly in that they had an extraordinarily deep love for their father. They always seemed happy to see him, greeting him with a warm embrace and kiss no matter how short the interval since they had last met. They called him 'Papa' at all

times. Whenever their father made a trip during the last war or in the years that followed, one of the three usually managed to arrange things so that she could go along.

If Churchill had a favourite it was probably Mary, the youngest, who resembles him more than did the other two. Though her features are heavier, she is the prettiest and most aristocratic-looking of the girls. She has neither the vivacity of Sarah nor the conversational gifts Diana had, but her serenity and quiet good humour were a delight to her father and are a joy to her friends. During the Churchills' last period of residence at 10 Downing Street, Mary's portrait by Sir Oswald Birley was side by side with his painting of her father in one of the large drawing-rooms. For most of Churchill's post-war years Mary and her husband, Christopher, lived with their children on one of the Chartwell farms only a few minutes' walk from the main house. Churchill often dropped in to see them on his rambles, and several times a week he would ask them over to lunch or dinner.

Churchill always secretly hoped that Sarah would also settle down at Chartwell. I remember driving with him one afternoon to a section of his estate overlooking the Weald of Kent. 'This,' he said rather sadly, 'is the spot I had picked out for Sarah. I'd like to build a house for her here.'

# CHAPTER TWELVE

# CHURCHILL

# AND AMERICA

CHURCHILL's supreme and abiding interest as a statesman was naturally the United Kingdom and the Commonwealth, but his love for France, and his admiration for and faith in the United States were unshakable and important parts of his character. The progress and destinies of other countries like Russia, Germany and Italy, of course, interested him, and at various stages in his career he had to become an expert on their affairs, but in his private conversation he seldom dwelt very long on any subject concerning countries other than America and France.

Few Englishmen of his day took such an interest in the United States or felt such an affinity for the country and its people. There was never a trace of anti-Americanism in any words I had ever heard him speak, although he spoke his mind freely and candidly when he disliked something the nation or an individual did. I cannot remember a time when he did not ask me some question about America. What were the strikes all about? What are they saying over there about this little country? Who is going to fill the vacancy on the Supreme Court? He liked to have a reasonably good answer to his questions, too, because he

was eager for information and during the years I knew him probably was not getting many reports. In the war years his hunger for good solid information about America was more than satisfied by the brilliant dispatches from the well-known Oxford don, Isaiah Berlin, who was attached to the British Embassy in Washington. It was Churchill's delight and satisfaction with these dispatches which caused him, during one of his visits to the U.S., to say to a secretary that he would like 'Berlin' to be asked to lunch. By now the story of how Irving Berlin, the song writer, turned up instead of Isaiah has gone around the world half a dozen times. Churchill was a little surprised by the appearance of the wrong Berlin at his luncheon table in the middle of the war, but the meeting turned out to be most agreeable for both.

Throughout the war and during his second Prime Ministership Churchill was, of course, in the closest and most intimate touch with America, first during the critical 'Cash and Carry' period, then Lend Lease and finally North Atlantic Treaty periods. At all times England needed and was receiving assistance from the United States, and it was Churchill's delicate task to maintain pride at home and extend gratitude across the Atlantic. Once or twice he talked to me a little about the problem of being on the receiving end of gifts from the United States. I remember him saying: 'One fact must always be remembered in dealing with Americans. They are the most generous people in all the world, and will not allow themselves to be *outdone* in generosity. Therefore a wise man will always show the greatest generosity towards his American friends.'

Because he felt so warmly towards America, Churchill frequently went out of his way to be accommodating. He

would receive visitors who really had no business to conduct or anything to contribute. A number of times I myself was guilty of asking him to see American friends of mine who merely wanted to shake the hand of the great man or be offered one of his cigars, and not once did he refuse. On visits to the United States he always held press conferences, though he could ill-afford the time and considered them such an ordeal that nothing ever induced him to hold one in England. He also accepted invitations to large dinner parties with his American publishers—something he never did in England. His best American friend was Bernard Baruch, the great financier and confidant of Presidents, whom Churchill knew for many years and with whom he stayed on most visits to New York. To my knowledge, Churchill never made a decision about an important personal matter affecting America without first getting Baruch's opinion, and he usually followed the advice of Bernie, as he called him. In New York Baruch tried to shelter Churchill from the thousands of people who wanted interviews, autographs and information, but Churchill never got much rest because he made so many dates himself and because Baruch himself always laid on some fairly large dinner or luncheon parties.

In England, the American Ambassadors were always welcome at Churchill's door and were treated with great kindness during the years I knew him. Of the more recent ones Lewis Douglas was probably the closest friend and the person Churchill enjoyed seeing most. Though he liked the late John Winant, who served during the difficult war years, Churchill found him a little heavy and sombre at times. Churchill also saw hundreds of American tourists and visitors every year. Gardner and Fleur Cowles, of *Look*

magazine, were regular luncheon guests at Chartwell, and when distinguished authors or journalists like Dorothy Thompson or Edward Murrow turned up in London they were either invited for a meal or a drink, or if they asked for an appointment they invariably got it.

When I first came to know Churchill, the President of the United States was Harry Truman. Their relations were excellent, and each held the other in high esteem. Churchill always regretted the fact that he did not fly to Washington shortly after Roosevelt's death in order to get to know Truman the moment he took office. 'Perhaps things would have been altogether different in Europe if we could have worked together from the start,' Churchill once told me. 'The last time I saw him Truman confessed that he didn't know very much during his first year in office. I might have helped him.'

The afternoon the message came through to Chartwell with the news that an attempt had been made to assassinate Truman, Churchill at once dictated a cable to Washington, then said to me: 'The President showed great courage. I'm so glad they didn't get him. I should think his standing in the country is higher than ever now.' I always felt that Churchill hoped Truman would run again in 1952 and be successful. He had scarcely heard of Stevenson before the campaign, and while he respected Eisenhower as a soldier he knew nothing of his abilities in the political fields. The idea of Taft becoming a candidate disturbed him considerably. Of all the Republicans that he knew he probably preferred Dewey, but when Eisenhower finally became the candidate Churchill wished him luck and carried in his pocket an 'I Like Ike' pin, which he would occasionally produce for the edification of an American guest. During

Eisenhower's first eighteen months as President, I cannot remember hearing Churchill mention him more than once or twice. I did not get the impression that relations were as intimate as he would have liked them to be. Of course, it is probably well known to Eisenhower that Churchill felt he should have acted with greater boldness and political acumen in the final stages of the conquest of Europe, that through his inflexibility of mind and purpose many opportunities to outsmart the Russians were missed. 'I tried my best to persuade Ike to take Berlin,' he said to me time and again, 'and to move as far east as possible, because I knew the Russians would make trouble in the end. But Eisenhower thought only of the military position. I couldn't get him or the others to consider the political problems which were as plain as day. I wanted to go to the Elbe in 1945, meet the Russians there, and settle the outstanding questions, but I couldn't get anyone to go with me.'

After his visit to Washington in 1954, however, Churchill felt much easier about his relationship with Eisenhower. When I saw him shortly after his return, still full of excitement, as he always was, from his journey, he said: 'Like Truman, Ike has learned a great deal since he took on this job. I found him to be quite a different man. We got along very well together.'

Churchill was out of office when the Korean war started, and it troubled him greatly that the United Kingdom was not contributing more manpower. 'I would have sent a brigade from Hong Kong the first thing had I been in charge,' he said to me one day. Once, when things were going badly for MacArthur, Churchill thought seriously of flying to Tokyo in a private plane to have a talk with the

General and offer his assistance. When the Inchon landings took place in 1951, he said: 'Now I must congratulate the Americans on the great victory. In MacArthur you have a great soldier, a great statesman and a great man. A brilliant move it was. You call it hit and run. I always called it a strike with a claw, but both come to the same thing.'

Anything that hurt Anglo-American relations drew a blast from Churchill. He deplored the anti-American attitude of Aneurin Bevan and some of his supporters, and he felt even stronger about the activities of Senator McCarthy. One day when McCarthy was reported as having said something particularly obnoxious, Churchill said in a tone of deep melancholy: 'As if we haven't enough problems without that fellow McCarthy pigging everything up.'

With the passing of Churchill, America has lost her greatest and most understanding friend in Europe.

Like most Englishmen, Churchill had an ambivalent attitude towards France. He loved the countryside and the food, and the light-hearted gaiety of the French people; but their political irresponsibility galled him, and he feared their moral weakness in a time of crisis. I recall one long dissertation on France in 1950, when I was down at Chartwell with a friend who had lived for a long time in Paris.

'The French are a broken people,' he said. 'The mainspring is gone. They've got neither a machine, nor a government, nor a leader. The trouble with France is its new constitution, which has given it nothing but an assembly. In France it's "for the assembly, by the assembly and of the assembly." France needs someone who can lead the people, who can get obedience—you must, you know,

have obedience sometimes. When I was in control of great power I, of course, didn't get my way all the time, and often when I did get it I had to work very hard. Questions had to be taken up with colleagues and associates. But after Roosevelt and I met everything was a lot easier. If we two agreed on a thing we usually got our way.'

Churchill was then silent, and no one said anything because he was obviously deep in thought. After a few minutes, looking very sad, he continued: 'But don't despair of the French. I have just been thinking of the last time I lunched out in Paris. It was at a little restaurant, and there were six or eight in our party. Nothing was planned before, so the affair couldn't have been more private. But word somehow passed from window to window and from door to door. Two hours later there was someone in every window of every house all the way back to the British Embassy. We could hardly make our way through the streets. Everyone was cheering. Now I'm not telling you all this to boast, but I do think that it shows that there is still some spirit among the French people.

'Not long ago I went to Nancy. They offered me the freedom of the city, so I thought I would go and accept it. Now Nancy is in the heart of the pro-German section of France and, of course, the city hall where I spoke has actually changed hands between German and French many, many times. The people there are pretty tired of war. But when I addressed the crowds from the balcony— in French, incidentally, and my French is something that has to be heard to be known—and said that my hope was to see a score of French divisions join a score of German divisions in a European army that would stand on guard against Communism, the ten thousand people threw their

arms in the air and cheered like anything. I thought this showed a pretty good spirit.

'A few days before that I was at Strasbourg attending the meeting of the Council of Europe. We passed before a guard of honour of French soldiers. They were smartly uniformed, their faces were strong and clean-cut, and when they marched they marched with vigour. Now I know a little about soldiers, and I would say that these soldiers were a match for any in the world.

'France will be all right. It's a blessed land. There aren't forty million people anywhere in the world living in such a rich land as France. I have faith in the French.'

# CHAPTER THIRTEEN

## CHURCHILL'S
## GREATNESS

THIS book has been my recollection of Churchill as I knew him, and in it I have tried to put down everything I can recall of that great man in the belief that even the most trivial bits of information about such a world figure will have value and interest. But now, looking back over these pages, I realize how little of the whole man I have in fact been able to depict, and particularly how little I have dwelt on those qualities which have made him one of the greatest men of this or any age.

For this I do not apologize. There will be many historical and political experts, far more qualified than I, who will pay fitting tribute to his political wisdom and statesmanship. They will have access to state papers. They will have known Churchill, as I did not, when his great mind was entirely occupied with affairs of state and statecraft. Their books will be able to give the true measure of his stature.

My meetings with Churchill were on a different plane. Though many of them were concerned with the weighty business of his *Memoirs*, they took place during his periods of relative relaxation, on his holidays or during weekend rests at Chartwell. There he was often able to slough off completely, as perhaps only a truly great man can do,

the cares of politics, and become something approaching an ordinary human being. It was always as a human being that I knew him—a genial, gregarious, sometimes crotchety but always lovable human being. It is of this man that I have written. And if the aura of greatness does not seem always to surround him, that is by no means a detraction from his genius. My view of him is necessarily limited.

Yet even in those moments of greatest ease and leisure, even in his most desultory table conversation, I, like all who approached him, was always aware of his inherent greatness. Everything about him was on a larger and grander scale than is customary in ordinary mortals. There was a certain *éclat* even in his pottering around the fish-pond or passing the port to a guest at dinner, for whatever he turned his attention to became, for the moment, lifted out of the commonplace.

When I was with him, though he talked often of politics and the great events of the day, he did so frequently more in a playful than a serious mood. But in all his conversation one could not help perceiving the flash of his quick imagination as it darted from thought to thought, his fascination with ideas, the breadth of his vision and the liveliness of his mind. While playing the genial host these qualities might be brought to bear on only the most trivial subjects. But they could also help to win a war and govern a great country.

His powers of concentration were prodigious. I never failed to be impressed by the way he could put his mind wholly to the question of the moment, whether it was an international crisis or the acquisition of a new tropical fish. He had that rare quality of seeming to be able to depart-mentalize his brain completely and open and shut the

doors of his knowledge at will. His mind was as orderly as his card table. When he painted, he painted to the exclusion of everything else. When he wrote his books, he became entirely the painstaking author. When he devoted himself to political questions, there was no one more deeply involved than he.

This remarkable power of concentration was joined to a fantastic memory and a vast appetite for hard work. What to lesser men might have been a lifetime's endeavour—namely, the production of six bulky volumes of his *Memoirs* —was to Churchill a spare-time project written while leading His Majesty's Opposition. And when he became Prime Minister again he still found time, old man though he was, to revise and complete the mammoth *History of the English Speaking Peoples*, which he had begun in 1929. Add to that his other great books, his painting, his momentous, carefully prepared speeches and broadcasts, all or most of them extra-curricular to the political career that has brought him his greatest glory, and he becomes a giant indeed.

These attributes of greatness were always apparent in Churchill, even in those off-duty moments when he was in his most relaxed and carefree mood. But what one felt perhaps most strongly of all was the impact of his vivid and extraordinary personality—his exuberant spirits, his fearlessness, his deep emotional capacity, his robust enjoyment of life and his stubborn refusal to compromise with the second-rate. He was English to the core, with an old-fashioned, swashbuckling Elizabethan Englishness that expressed itself at all times grandly and without petty restraint.

Therein, I think, lay much of the secret of his greatness,

and of the power he has had to capture the admiration and affection of the whole world. He was the epitome of all that was best in the English character. He possessed to a remarkable degree its loyalty and stubbornness, its courage against odds and its single-minded devotion to duty. He was John Bull himself, the true English bulldog. And those immense additional gifts—the superb power of his eloquence and his magnificent flair for showmanship— enabled him, especially in times of danger, to endue the whole nation with these qualities, and, at all times, to inspire his countrymen even when he did not convince them. He was one of the most remarkable characters the world has seen for generations, a great statesman, a great literary figure and a great personality with an insatiable zest and gusto and joy of living. He was a fascinating, lovable, brilliant, fabulous character, and with his death much of its savour has gone from the world.

Mr Churchill talked to me about death on a number of occasions, and I formed the impression that towards the end he was much more ready for it than he was earlier. Once he said to me: 'I look forward to dying. Sleep, endless, wonderful sleep—on a purple, velvety cushion. Every so often I will wake up, turn over, and go to sleep again.'

Another time, a few years before he died he said: 'I have no fear of death and the judgment. When I reach the Holy Gates I am confident that St Peter will be glad to see me. It might be said that perhaps I have sometimes eaten and drunk too well, but on balance I think I shall qualify for entry.'

*My dear*
# MISTER
# CHURCHILL

To
My dear
Mr & Mrs George

from

Walter Graebner

London

March 26
1965